Chemistry on a Budget:

Labs Using Supplies From Local Stores

by Marjorie R. Heesemann

Copyright 2013. All rights reserved.
ISBN 978-0-578-12915-0

Dedication

To all the students I have taught over the years -- they have challenged me to keep improving as a teacher.

Acknowledgements

Thanks to the many teachers I've worked with over the years for their tremendous generosity and advice, especially the science department at Greenwich High School in Greenwich, Connecticut, and my fellow chemistry teachers Arleene Ferko, Ray Hamilton and Bruce McFadden.

Thanks to Mary G. Merritt, Ingrid Steffensen and Jeff Bruce for their advice and encouragement.

Thanks to Reann Sponable for providing a student's perspective while reading these labs; to Colleen Meyer, Gail Meyer and Steve Shope for their help, encouragement and illustrations; and, to Timmy Louer for the excellent cover photograph!

Table of Contents

Introduction — Pages 1-3

Laboratory Safety — Pages 4-5

Lab 1: Thickness of Aluminum Foil — Pages 6-13

    Lab Pages for "Thickness of Aluminum Foil":
- 10 question report: pages 9-10
- Full lab-writeup: pages 12-13

Lab 2: Density, Two Methods — Pages 14-21

    Lab Pages for "Density, Two Methods":
- 10 question report: pages 17-18
- Full lab-writeup: pages 20-21

Lab 3: Density of Three Liquids — Pages 22-29

    Lab Pages for "Density of Three Liquids":
- 10 question report: pages 25-26
- Full write-up: pages 28-29

Lab 4: Analysis of a Mixture — Pages 30-37

    Lab Pages for "Analysis of a Mixture":
- 10 question report: pages 33-34
- Full write-up: page 36-37

Lab 5: Paper Chromatography — Pages 38-48

    Lab Pages for "Paper Chromatography":
- 10 question report: pages 42-43 plus a data chart on page 44
- Full write-up: pages 46-47 plus a data chart on page 48

Lab 6: Catching Moles — Pages 49-56

    Lab Pages for "Catching Moles:
- 10 question report: pages 52-53
- Full write-up: pages 55-56

Lab 7: Moles in Your Name?   Pages 57-62

    Lab Pages for "Moles in Your Name?":
- 10 question report: page 60
- Full write-up: page 62

Lab 8: A Chemical Reaction   Pages 63-72

    Lab Pages for "A Chemical Reaction":
- 10 question report: pages 68-69
- Full write-up: pages 71-72

Lab 9 Molar Volume   Pages: 73-81

    Lab Pages for "Molar Volume":
- 10 question report: pages 77-78
- Full write-up: pages 80-81

Lab 10: Heat of Fusion   Pages 82-89

    Lab Pages for "Heat of Fusion":
- 10 question report: pages 85-86
- Full write-up: pages 88-89

Lab 11: Calorimetry   Pages 90-99

    Pages to use for "Calorimetry":
- 10 question report: pages 93-94 and 95 for a data page
- Full write-up: pages 97-98 and 99 for a data page

Lab 12: Household Acids & Bases   Pages 100-110

    Lab Pages for "Household Acids & Bases":
- 10 question report: page 103 only, and data tables on pages 104-105
- Full write-up: page 108 only, and data tables on pages 109-110

Lab 13: Preparing pH indicators   Pages 111-115

    Lab Pages for "Preparing pH Indicators":
- Page 115 for a simple lab report

Lab 14: Coinium   Pages 116-123

    Lab Pages for "Coinium":
- 10 question report: pages 119-120
- Full write-up: pages 122-123

Lab 15: Preparing a Cross-Linked Polymer   Pages 124-131

    Lab Pages for "Preparing a Cross-Linked Polymer":
- 10 question report: pages 127-128
- Full writeup: pages 130-131

Lab 16: Salt and Ice Cream?   Pages 132-140

    Lab Pages for "Salt in Ice Cream?":
- 10 question report: pages 136-137
- Full writeup: pages 139-140

Postlogue and About the Author   Page 141

Index   Pages 142-143

Introduction

Teaching high school chemistry for fifteen years, I had encountered a great variety of laboratory activities. Recently, I taught at a small school where I did not have the funds to order chemicals or materials. I had to use what was in the lab and buy other supplies I needed at local stores.

During that year, my chemistry teaching knowledge was used to its greatest extent as I figured out ways to find activities and purchase the supplies I needed at a reasonable price. It was tough and I considered myself very fortunate to have a variety of labs readily available in my personal teaching files.

A teacher new to a school doesn't usually have science department budget money to finance class activities. By the summer, the funds available have already been used to purchase materials or are allocated for other purposes. At the end of that challenging school year, I realized that not everyone has experienced so many laboratory activities and I wanted to share chemistry labs for the teacher with limited supplies and funds.

The labs contained here are designed for a classroom that has a water supply, access to ice, beakers, test tubes, stirring rods, graduated cylinders, thermometers, rulers, and a laboratory balance (electric or triple beam). You will have to purchase extra supplies at locations such as a grocery store, dollar store, craft store, or general-goods store. Some supplies can be ordered on the Internet.

Each lab contains the following:

1) An Introduction with recommendations specific to the lab, including a corresponding ChemMatters article for classroom use;

2) A two-page lab where the student produces a report answering 10 questions;

3) Answers to that lab's 10 questions; and,

4) A two-page lab where the student writes a full-laboratory report.

Both the 10-question format and the full-lab report format are two pages in length so the teacher can photocopy a single, two-sided lab handout and use less paper.

If more space is required for data, students can draw a lab table on their own paper or the teacher can photocopy the specialized data pages provided.

ChemMatters Articles

"ChemMatters" magazine is a publication produced by the American Chemical Society written for use in the high school chemistry classroom. It contains articles about various phenomena and explains the chemistry behind them. It is a great supplement and shows a variety of real world applications of chemistry.

For each lab, I have identified a ChemMatters supplementary article that can be printed from the Internet. Directions are below.

1) Enter one of the following links:

   http://portal.acs.org/portal/acs/corg/content/ or http://redirect.acs.org/404.html

2) Enter "ChemMatters magazine" in the Search box at the top right.

3) Click on "ChemMatters Magazine" – it should be the first listing in the Search Results.

4) Click on "Past Issues" – it should be down the page (about halfway) and the fourth choice across the listing.

   From the listing, find the issue you're looking for.

Or, if you desire, there is a direct link:

http://portal.acs.org/portal/acs/corg/content?_nfpb=true&_pageLabel=PP_SUPERARTICLE&node_id=2119&use_sec=false&sec_url_var=region1

You may want to bookmark this link once you get to the page.

If you're having difficulty finding an article, try using the "Search" box at the top right.

Materials Sign-Out

If you want to make sure that students return certain lab materials intact, you can have them sign them out. Students tend to be more careful if they know an item is their responsibility (ex. butane lighters for Molar Volume lab). A sample sign out sheet might be:

Student Name	Item	Signed out	Returned

Students turn in lab materials individually and the teacher can initial the "Signed out" and "Returned" column. This aids in identifying the students damaging laboratory materials or not returning them at all. Variations of this sign out sheet could be used for other classroom items such as calculators.

Extra Credit Ideas

Students are always looking for ways to earn extra credit. In my class, students have a Class Participation grade for the quarter. Over the years it became based on class attendance and behavior – I informed the students that they all started with a Class Participation grade of 100 and it went down when they cut class, were tardy, or were a disciplinary problem and received detention. It was a way to encourage and reward positive behavior. Students could earn back participation points lost due to tardiness by serving detention – 15 minutes for each 5 point deduction. Participation points lost for cutting class or discipline issues could not be earned back. All of this was recorded in my class attendance book to make it easier to calculate the Class Participation grade.

I found a **Lab Cleanup Day** was useful in getting jobs completed in the lab such as cleaning glassware, labeling new lab materials or hanging posters. I recommend that the teacher (a) plan tasks in advance because it's hard to think of them on the spot, and (b) determine time amounts for each task to make it easier to determine the time/points earned for each task. I found that students appreciated the chance to earn extra credit and would take pride in their classroom. Pretty soon students will be asking for cleanup days!

Lab Assistant

A student who has been absent from a lab activity usually must perform it after school with the teacher supervising. The student is alone and the teacher ends up being the lab partner. Bruce McFadden, a chemistry teacher at Staples High School in Westport, Connecticut shared his technique for this situation.

To earn extra credit on the lab, another student who had previously performed it acts as a **Lab Assistant** and is the lab partner for the absent student. Since the student Lab Assistant has already completed the activity, it is not necessary to reteach the lab lesson but simply to supervise the two students performing the lab. The student earning the extra credit would write *Lab Assistant* at the top of the lab. I found the Lab Assistants to be very enthusiastic and appreciated the chance to earn extra credit. I highly recommend it!

Laboratory Safety

It is very important to teach your students chemistry laboratory safety at the beginning of the school year. Don't perform a lab that uses chemicals or laboratory burners until you have taught about lab safety and have lab safety contracts signed by students and their parents.

The Laboratory Safety Contract shows that you taught chemistry laboratory safety and reflects a pattern of safety education in your classroom lab. Lab accidents have the potential for lawsuits, and even though the school's insurance policy should cover the teacher, instructors still can be sued individually. It is in your best interest to have a "trail of safety" throughout the school year. Start the year with safety instruction, highlight lab safety for every laboratory lesson, and include specific lab safety instructions in every laboratory handout.

Fewer lab accidents occur with teachers with more experience. I recall a lab accident during my first year teaching. A student's water bath collapsed (ring stand, ring and beaker over a Bunsen burner) and the hot water spilled on him. I rushed to his aid but he said he was okay, "My lab apron protected me." I cannot emphasize enough the importance of safety equipment, eye goggles and rubberized lab aprons; and, the teacher must enforce their proper use.

Years later my class was performing a lab using hydrochloric acid and mossy zinc to produce hydrogen gas. The plastic container for the reaction had one small hole for the gas to escape. This hole was accidentally stoppered and the gas could not escape. The gas pressure built up in the plastic bottle and it eventually exploded, spraying hydrochloric acid on the student and his lab partner. I can still see the acid dripping off one student's safety goggles – the goggles had protected his eyes from a horrible accident. The two students involved just washed the acid from their goggles, aprons and hands. What a scary moment!

A lab class can include from 24 to 30 students – I have been fortunate to work at schools concerned with laboratory safety that limited chemistry class size to 24 students; however, I have also had a class that grew to 29 one year. I'm sure there are classes that are bigger in U.S. schools which is why teaching laboratory safety is even more important. Your students must have the knowledge of how to work safely, for themselves, their fellow students and the teacher.

In lab, it is important that the students are protected – physically, with knowledge of how to act safely in the lab, and with knowledge of how to use safety equipment in an emergency.

Sources:

http://pubs.acs.org/doi/abs/10.1021/ed024p354

http://www.cdc.gov/niosh/docs/2007-107/pdfs/2007-107.pdf

http://chemlabs.uoregon.edu/Safety/GeneralInstructions.html

http://www.files.chem.vt.edu/RVGS/ACT/lab/safety_rules.html

http://www.ou.edu/oupd/labfire.htm

http://www3.nsta.org/main/news/pdf/tst9909_36.pdf

http://www.nsta.org/pdfs/free/tst_CrowleyWarren.pdf

http://www.kirkwood.k12.mo.us/parent_student/khs/taysish/assignmentshandouts/reactions/ROCKET0708.pdf

Vos, Robert and Pell, Sarah W.J. (1990). "Limiting Lab Liability: Protect Yourself and Your Students," The Science Teacher. 57(9): 34-38.

Heesemann, Marjorie R. (1992). "Liability Issues for the School Chemistry Laboratory", Project for Master of Education Degree in Science Education, Department of Learning and Instruction, Graduate School of Education, University at Buffalo.

http://daphne.palomar.edu/safetyquiz/safetyquiz.htm
An online quiz which produces a Certificate of Completion with a score on the quiz.

http://www.labsafetyinstitute.org/
A good resource.

Lab: Thickness of Aluminum Foil

Summary
Student measures the mass, length and width of a piece of aluminum foil. Using the formulas for density and volume, the thickness of the aluminum foil sample is calculated.

One student measures two samples and shares the data. Each student pair ends up with a total of four sets of data.

Student Skills:
Significant figures – both in measurement and calculations
Scientific notation

Lab: Thickness of Aluminum Foil   Teacher Information Page

Background:
This is a good introductory lab for those first few days of school where shortened class periods are typical. Also, this lab helps illustrate the importance of significant figures, an abstract idea.

Class Materials:
Aluminum foil   Ruler   Balance

Materials for the Teacher:
Scissors   Permanent marker

Preparation:
Cut out and label squares of aluminum foil – vary the sizes and try to use the same roll of aluminum foil.

During Lab:
Circulate to observe and aid students.

Calculating the thickness of the foil is shown in two separate steps to reduce student confusion.

Hints:

If you have the class time, you can have the students cut out their own aluminum foil samples; or, you can cut out and label the samples ahead of time (12 to 20) and request that students not damage them.

You might want to use a sign-out sheet to encourage returning the materials in good condition. For those who damage the foil samples, an appropriate consequence could be coming in after school and cutting out more samples.

Pages to use for "Thickness of Aluminum Foil" lab:
10 question report: pages 9-10.
Full write-up: pages 12-13.

Possible ChemMatters article:
Brownlee, Christen, "Super Fibers" pp.11-13, February, 2006 ChemMatters, American Chemical Society

This article discusses the *nanotube*, another object too small to measure with regular laboratory instruments.

This article is also a good supplement for the topic of **Covalent Bonding**.

Directions of how to get the article online are on Page 2.

Sources:

http://www.brighthub.com/education/k-12/articles/8105.aspx

Chapter 1 Science Skills Consumer Lab
© Pearson Education, Inc., publishing as Pearson Prentice Hall. All rights reserved.
Physical Science Lab Manual - Chapter 1 Consumer Lab 281.

http://www.windsorct.org/whscondon/documents/DensityLab.doc

http://en.wikipedia.org/wiki/Accuracy_and_precision#Accuracy_versus_precision:_the_target_analogy

Addison-Wesley Chemistry @ 2000 by Prentice Hall, Inc.

Brownlee, Christen, "Super Fibers" p.11, February, 2006 ChemMatters, American Chemical Society.

Lab: Thickness of Aluminum Foil   Name _____

Purpose: To measure the thickness of aluminum foil indirectly using its density and volume.

Because aluminum foil is so thin, the thickness value will be very small. This is a situation where it is important to apply the rules for significant figures to the measurements and the calculations.

Materials:
Aluminum foil samples   Ruler   Balance

Procedure:
Measure the mass, length, and width for two different foil samples. Share your results with another student.

Measure as accurately as your instruments allow!

Data

Sample #	Mass (g)	Volume (cm³)	Length (cm)	Width (cm)	Thickness (cm)

Calculations
It is important to apply significant figure rules for multiplying and dividing, that the result is rounded to the lowest number of significant figures in the measurements.

1) Volume of the aluminum foil sample

   Density = Mass / Volume,

   D = M / V → D x V = M → **V = M / D**

   The density of aluminum is 2.699 g/cm³.

2) Thickness of the aluminum foil sample

   Volume = Length x Width x Height (or Thickness)

   V = L x W x T → **T = V / (L x W)**

Questions

Answer these questions on your own paper using full sentences – either rewrite the question or incorporate it into your answer.

1. Calculate the Volume and the Thickness for one of the samples. Include the identity of the sample, the formula used, the mathematical solution and the answer with units.

2. Explain why you couldn't just use a centimeter ruler to measure the thickness of the aluminum foil.

3. Explain why it is incorrect to have recorded a length of the aluminum foil square as 3.4575 cm after measuring with a ruler marked to the nearest millimeter.

4. Explain why scientists use significant figures when taking measurements and completing calculations in the laboratory.

5. Describe one time that a number is exempt from the use of significant figures.

6. How many of your measured values had the same thickness (the samples had the first two non-zero digits matching)? Include the sample numbers and thickness values in your answer.

7. Calculate the average thickness of your samples. Show your work.

8. Evaluate the quality of your results.

9. Describe how you would improve this lab using the same materials.

10. A very thin layer of gold plating was placed on a metal tray that measured 25.22 cm by 13.22 cm. The gold plating increased the mass of the plate by 0.0512 g. Given that the density of gold is 19.32 g/cm^3, calculate the thickness of the gold plating. Show your work including units.

Answer Key to "Thickness of Aluminum Foil":

1. Sample calculation: Sample #3:

   Mass = 0.025 g   Length = 10.00 cm   Width = 5.00 cm

   V = M / D = 0.025 g / 2.699 g/cm^3 = 0.0093 cm^3

   T = V / (L x W) = 0.0093 cm^3 / (10.00 cm x 5.00 cm) = 0.00019 cm or 1.9 x 10^{-4} cm

2. The aluminum foil thickness came out to be 0.00019cm. The ruler only measures to 0.01 cm and could not measure this value accurately.

3. When marked to the nearest millimeter, the ruler only measures to ±0.01 cm. Any extra numbers are not a result of measuring with that instrument.

4. The significant figures in a measurement show the accuracy of the measurement instrument. For example, measurements reported as 15 grams versus 15.00 grams could be the same object measured on different balance.

5. A number is exempt from the use of significant digits (or has an infinite number of significant figures) when they are **definitions,** not measurements. For example, 100 cm = 1 m = 0.001 km

6. Answer dependent on sample data.

7. Answer dependent on sample data.

8. Several answers apply. One possibility is concern about the quality of the foil sample measured, either how square or how flat the sample is (if it is wrinkled from many uses).

9. Several answers apply. One possibility is using a fresh sample that has not been precut and does not have wrinkles.

10. Volume of the gold foil sample

    V = M / D = 0.0512 g / 19.32 g/cm^3 = 0.00265 cm^3

    Thickness of the gold foil sample

    T = V / (L x W) = 0.00265 cm^3 / (25.22 cm x 13.22 cm) = 0.00000795 cm = 7.95 x 10^{-6} cm

    The rule for significant figure calculations is to not round between similar operations (in this case, multiplying and dividing).

Lab: Thickness of Aluminum Foil   Name _____

Purpose: To measure the thickness of aluminum foil indirectly using its density and volume.

Because aluminum foil is so thin, the thickness value will be very small. This is a situation where it is important to apply the rules for significant figures to the measurements and the calculations.

Materials:
Aluminum foil samples   Ruler   Balance

Procedure:
Measure the mass, length, and width for two different foil samples. Share your results with another student.

Measure as accurately as your instruments allow!

Data

Sample #	Mass (g)	Volume (cm^3)	Length (cm)	Width (cm)	Thickness (cm)

Calculations

It is important to apply significant figure rules for multiplying and dividing, that the result is rounded to the lowest number of significant figures in the measurements.

1) Volume of the aluminum foil sample

   Density = Mass / Volume
   D = M / V → D x V = M → **V = M / D**

   The density of aluminum is 2.699 g/cm^3.

2) Thickness of the aluminum foil sample

   Volume = Length x Width x Height (or Thickness)

   V = L x W x T → **T = V / (L x W)**

Laboratory Report Requirements

Label and skip a line between each section. Data tables and charts attached on separate pages are to be labeled (ex. Data Table – see attached)

Title

Purpose

Materials

Procedure

Data

Sample Calculation
Show a sample calculation for Volume and Thickness for one trial. Calculate and collect the remaining results in the table provided.

For each sample calculation, include the identity of the sample, formula used, the calculation and answer with units.

Conclusion
In paragraph form, discuss the following ideas:

- Calculate the average thickness of your samples, showing your work. Evaluate the accuracy of this thickness average.

- How many samples had the same thickness (the first two non-zero digits matching)? List those samples and thickness values.

- Evaluate the quality of your results.

- Describe how you would improve this lab using the same or similar materials.

Lab: Density, Two Methods

Summary
Part 1: Student measures mass, length, width and height of a regular-shaped object and calculates the object's volume and density.

Part 2: Student measures mass and volume of an irregularly shaped object using water displacement and calculates the object's density.

Student Skills:
Measuring mass and volume to calculate density
Using water-displacement to measure the volume of an object with an irregular shape

Lab: Density, Two Methods — Teacher Information Page

Background:
This laboratory is basic because density is a property that can aid in identifying a substance. Also, this lab does not involve a chemical reaction so you have more time to teach laboratory safety before performing labs with chemicals or fire.

The density of a regular-shaped object is easy to measure. The main challenge is getting enough items to test. Wooden or plastic blocks from the toy section of a store or styrofoam cubes cut from larger pieces could be used. I recommend that the items be labeled to identify them later in the lab report.

For irregular-shaped objects, almost anything can be used, just items you don't mind getting wet, that don't absorb the water, and are narrow enough to be put into a graduated cylinder. I have used dice, screws or nails, toy models, marbles and stones. Once you have gathered items for one lab you can store them and use them the next year.

Class Materials:
Rulers (centimeter)
Balances
Graduated cylinders
Access to water
Regular-shaped objects
Irregular-shaped objects

Materials for the teacher:
Nothing past the class materials.

Preparation:
Gather materials. You may wish to set up stations around the room (depending on the number of balances available) and have the students move to another station after measuring.

During lab:
Monitor student progress and aid where appropriate.

Pages to use for "Density, Two Methods":
10 question report: pages 17-18.
Full lab-write-up: pages 20-21.

Possible ChemMatters article:
Caruana, Claudia M., "Anesthesia: Chemistry in the Operating Room," ChemMatters, February, 2010, pp.8-9, American Chemical Society.

This article presents a brief history of anesthesia used for surgery and dentistry.

Directions of how to get the article online are on Page 2.

Another option is a ChemMatters article on the CD ROM, but not online:
Becker, Robert, "Question from the Classroom: A Royal Rip-off!", ChemMatters, February, 2001, p.2, American Chemical Society

This article explains how Archimedes used density and the displacement of water to prove a king's crown was not pure gold.

Sources:

http://www.kwanga.net/chemnotes/density-lab.pdf

http://teachers.oregon.k12.wi.us/ehrlich/For%20the%20Love%20of%20Money/Penny%20Density%20Lab.pdf

http://chemistry.about.com/od/chemistrylabexperiments/qt/meniscus.htm

Caruana, Claudia M., "Anesthesia: Chemistry in the Operating Room," ChemMatters, February, 2010, pp.8-9, American Chemical Society.

Becker, Robert, "Question from the Classroom: A Royal Rip-off!", ChemMatters, February, 2001, p.2, American Chemical Society

Lab: Density, Two Methods

Name _____

Purpose:
To measure mass and volume to calculate density.
To use water-displacement to measure the volume of an object with an irregular shape.

Materials:
Ruler   Balance   Graduated cylinder

Remember significant figures when measuring!

Procedure One:
Identify three regular-shaped objects made of the same material.
For each object, measure its mass, length, width and height.

Object	Mass (g)	Length (cm)	Width (cm)	Height (cm)	Density (g/cm^3)

Procedure Two:
Identify three irregularly-shaped objects made of the same material.
For each object, measure its mass and its volume using water displacement.

Object	Mass (g)	Volume of object in water (mL)	Volume of water (mL)	Volume of object (mL)	Density (g/mL)

Calculations

Procedure One:

Volume = Length x width x height

Procedure Two:

Volume of object = volume of object & water − volume of water

For both procedures:

Density = mass / volume

Questions
Answer these questions on your own paper using full sentences – either rewrite the question or incorporate it into your answer.

1. Calculate the volume of one regular shaped object that was measured. Identify the sample, show the formula used and show the calculation and the answer including units.

2. Calculate the volume of one irregular-shaped that was measured. Identify the sample, show the formula used, and show the calculation and the answer including units.

3. Calculate the density of one object measured. Identify which object, write the formula used, and show the calculation and the answer including units.

4. Explain why a pure substance always has the same density regardless of the size of the sample.

5. State the definition of **meniscus**. Explain how to consistently measure liquid volume.

6. Describe briefly the method of **water displacement** to measure the volume of an object.

7. Describe the strengths and weaknesses of using density to identify substances in lab.

8. Based on your previous experiences, list the following substances in order from the lowest density to the highest. Explain your reasoning.
   lead pipe, water, pine 2" X 4" board, styrofoam pieces.

9. Evaluate the quality of your results.

10. Describe how you would improve this lab using the same or similar materials.

Answer Key to "Density, Two Methods":

Questions 1-3 are answered using sample data.

1. Volume = Length x width x height
   Volume = 10.00 cm x 4.00 cm x 2.00 cm = 80.0 cm^3

2. Volume of object = volume of object & water – volume of water
   Volume = 70.00 mL – 50.00 mL = 20.00 mL

3. Density = mass / volume
   Density = 30.00 g / 20.00 mL = 1.500 g/mL

4. A pure substance is defined as having constant composition throughout. Examples include elements and compounds.

5. A **meniscus** is the curve at the top of a sample of liquid produced by the attraction of the liquid for the walls of the container. Read the measurement so that the line you are reading is even with the center of the meniscus. This can required bending down so that your eye is even with the top of the liquid being measured.

6. Put enough water in a graduated cylinder to cover the object when submerged. Measure the water (at the bottom of the meniscus). Carefully, place the object in the graduated cylinder. Measure the water and object. Subtract the two measurements to determine the volume of the object.

7. Because density is an intensive property and is the same for any sample of a pure substance, it is an easy way to discriminate between samples with similar physical properties. It is limited because the sample may not be a pure substance.

8. Lowest density to highest:
   Styrofoam pieces, pine 2" x 4" board, water, lead pipe
   Explanations will vary.

9. Several answers apply. One possibility is that the density values did not match and that not enough samples were measured.

10. Several answers apply. One possibility is to be sure to place the object in the water carefully so it is not splashed out of the graduated cylinder (or on the sides).

Lab: Density, Two Methods

Purpose:
To measure mass and volume to calculate density.
To use water-displacement to measure the volume of an object with an irregular shape.

Materials:
Ruler   Balance   Graduated cylinder

Remember significant figures when measuring!

Procedure One:
Identify three regular-shaped objects made of the same material.
For each object, measure its mass, length, width and height.

Object	Mass (g)	Length (cm)	Width (cm)	Height (cm)	Density (g/cm^3)

Procedure Two:
Identify three irregularly-shaped objects made of the same material.
For each object, measure its mass and its volume using water displacement.

Object	Mass (g)	Volume of object in water (mL)	Volume of water (mL)	Volume of object (mL)	Density (g/mL)

Calculations

Procedure One:

Volume = Length x width x height

Procedure Two:

Volume of object = volume of object & water – volume of water

For both procedures:

Density = mass / volume

Laboratory Report Requirements

Label and skip a line between each section. Data tables and charts attached on separate pages are to be labeled (ex. Data Table – see attached).

Title

Purpose

Materials

Procedure

Data

Sample Calculation
Show a sample calculation for one trial of a regular-shaped object and another for one trial of an irregular-shaped object. Calculate and collect the remaining results in the table provided.

For a Sample Calculation, include the identity of the sample, the formula used, and show the calculation and answer including units.

Conclusion
In paragraph form, discuss the following ideas:

- Explain why a pure substance always has the same density no matter what size sample is measured.

- Describe the strengths and weaknesses of using density to identify substances in lab.

- Evaluate the quality of your results.

- Describe how you would improve this lab using the same or similar materials.

Lab: Density of Three Liquids

Summary
Student measures mass and volume of a liquid sample. The volume of the liquid is increased and mass and volume are recorded five more times. The data is used to prepare a graph. A total of three different liquids are tested.

Student Skills:
Graphing of laboratory data to produce a best-fit line
Calculating the slope of a graphed line

Lab: Density of Three Liquids — Teacher Information Page

Background

This is another good introductory lab. Some labs I researched use viscous liquids such as molasses and antifreeze for liquids denser than water but they pose cleanup problems. I chose using a saturated salt solution because it's easy to prepare and easy for the students to clean out of graduate cylinders.

I recommend using a large container of each liquid -- students can fill their beaker or cup from it and bring the sample back to their lab station. Some possible large containers are a clean, empty 2-liter bottle or a large 1000 mL beaker.

Class Materials:
Graduated cylinders
Access to a balance
Access to water
3 liquids provided by the teacher
Paper toweling
Beakers or cups to hold approximately 25 ml of liquid

Materials for the teacher:
Isopropyl (rubbing) alcohol
Water
Saturated salt solution
Food Coloring (optional)

Preparation:

The three liquids must be placed in dispensing containers. If you choose, add one or two drops of food coloring to each main container to make it easier to tell the liquids apart.

Hint

Some sources instruct to rinse the graduate cylinder with alcohol and let it evaporate. This evaporation takes time which is precious during a laboratory period. Typical school-supplied brown paper towels do not absorb liquid quickly, and using too much towel can result in it getting stuck in the bottom of a graduate cylinder. Ugh...

A technique to use this toweling effectively was shared with me by Ray Hamilton at Greenwich High School in Greenwich, Connecticut. Take a piece of paper towel about 4" x 10". Fold it in half length-wise; then, fold it in half again. Now you have a long column of towel that you can lower into the graduate cylinder to blot the liquid on the bottom without it getting stuck. If the towel starts to bend, fold it around a stirring rod to keep it straight.

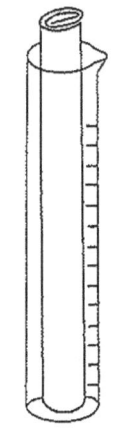

During lab:
Monitor student progress and aid where appropriate.

Pages to use for "Density of Three Liquids":
10 question report: pages 25-26.

Full write-up: pages 28-29.

Possible ChemMatters article:
Cardulla, Frank, "Alien Atmospheres: There's No Place Like Home," ChemMatters, October, 2003, pp. 9-11, American Chemical Society.

This article compares the atmospheres of Earth's two closest planets, Venus and Mars.

This article is also a good supplement for the topic of **Gases** and **Atmospheric Pressure**.

Directions of how to get the article online are on Page 2.

Another option is a ChemMatters article on the CD ROM, but not online:
Becker, Robert, "Cartesian Divers: Squeeze Play!", ChemMatters, February, 2001, pp.4-6, American Chemical Society.
This article shows how a Cartesian diver works and how to make one.

Sources:

https://www.msu.edu/~moorean4/TestSite/Chemistry%20Labs/Unit%202%20Labs/densityofliquids.pdf

http://www.edinformatics.com/science_projects/labs/density_lab2.htm

http://www.tuckahoe.k12.ny.us/Science%20pdfs/Oceans/ds%20Density%20Lab.pdf

http://paws.wcu.edu/jclement/140prepmanual.pdf

http://chemistry.about.com/od/chemistrylab/a/How-To-Dry-A-Graduated-Cylinder.htm

http://haventeam.com/betsie/parser.cgi/0005/chemistry.about.com/od/chemistrylab/a/How-To-Dry-A-Graduated-Cylinder.htm

http://chemistry.about.com/od/chemistrylab/a/How-To-Dry-A-Graduated-Cylinder.htm

Dorin, et al., Chemistry @1987, Allyn and Bacon, Inc.

Cardulla, Frank, "Alien Atmospheres: There's No Place Like Home," ChemMatters, October, 2003, pp. 9-11, American Chemical Society.

Becker, Robert, "Cartesian Divers: Squeeze Play!", ChemMatters, February, 2001, pp.4-6, American Chemical Society.

Lab: Density of Three Liquids   Name: _____

Purpose:
To measure the mass and volume of various liquid samples.
To graph the data and observe the relationship between the slope and density.

Materials:
Graduated cylinder   Balance
3 liquids provided by the teacher   Beaker or cup

Procedure:
1. Determine the mass of a clean, dry graduated cylinder.
2. Obtain approximately 30 mL of the liquid being measured in a small cup or beaker.
3. Add approximately 5 mL of the liquid to the graduated cylinder. Dry the outside if you have spilled any liquid. Record the volume of the liquid. Determine the mass of the cylinder with the liquid in it and record.
4. Add 5 mL more of the liquid to the cylinder, recording the mass and volume after each addition. Continue until you have completed 6 measurements.
5. Discard the liquid. Rinse and dry the beaker and the graduate cylinder between liquids. Measure three different liquids.

Calculations
Density = mass / volume   Remember significant figure rules!

Graph
Graph Mass vs. Volume (y vs. x) for all three sets of data on a single set of axes.
Plot the points for one liquid, and then draw a best-fit line that goes through the 0, 0 point.
Complete one line before drawing the next data line.

Questions
Answer these questions on your own paper using full sentences -- rewrite the question or incorporate it into your answer.
1. Provide a sample calculation of density for one trial only. Include identity of the sample, formula used, calculation and answer with units.
2. For each of the three liquids, calculate the average density based on the measurements. Show your work.
3. For each of the three liquids, calculate the slope of the graph. Show your work.
4. Compare the average density values to the slopes of the corresponding graphs. How close were the values?
5. Evaluate the quality of your results.
6. Calculate the percent error of the average density for water based on your lab measurements.
7. Describe how you would improve this lab using the same or similar materials.
8. The mass of an empty graduated cylinder is 70 grams. When it is filled with 50 ml of liquid its mass is 120 grams. a) What is the mass of just the liquid? b) What is the density of the liquid? Show work for all calculations.
9. Oil does not mix with water. When an oil tanker spills, the oil floats on the surface of the ocean. Why does oil float and not sink?
10. There is water in the pan of Tommy's and Tina's balance but they ignore it while measuring the mass of a liquid. What effect does this have on their measurements and density results?

Data: Liquid 1 - Water

Sample	Mass of water and cylinder (g)	Mass of dry cylinder (g)	Mass of Water (g)	Volume of Water (mL)	Density (g/mL)
1	------------------	------------------	0	0	-------------
2					
3					
4					
5					
6					
7					

Data: Liquid 2 – Alcohol

Sample	Mass of water and cylinder (g)	Mass of dry cylinder (g)	Mass of Water (g)	Volume of Water (mL)	Density (g/mL)
1	------------------	------------------	0	0	-------------
2					
3					
4					
5					
6					
7					

Data: Liquid 3 – Salt Water

Sample	Mass of water and cylinder (g)	Mass of dry cylinder (g)	Mass of Water (g)	Volume of Water (mL)	Density (g/mL)
1	------------------	------------------	0	0	-------------
2					
3					
4					
5					
6					
7					

Answer Key for "Density of Three Liquids":

1. For example:

    Liquid 1 – Sample #2

    Mass of water + cylinder = 15.00 g

    − Mass of cylinder = 5.00 g

    Mass of water = 10.00 g   Volume of water = 10.00 ml

    Density = Mass / Volume = 10.00 g / 10.00 ml = 1.000 g/ml

2. Answer dependent on student data.
    Average density = Σ 6 density values / 6

3. Answer dependent on student data.
    Slope = Δy / Δx using two points from the best-fit line.

4. Ideally, the average density values would be close to/equal to the slope of the best-fit line.

5. Answer dependent on student results.

6. Sample data: measured value = 1.25 g/ml   accepted value = 1.00 g/ml
    % error = | measured value − accepted value | / accepted value x 100%
    % error = | 1.25 g/ml − 1.00 g/ml | / 1.00 g/mL x 100%
    = 0.25 g/ml / 1.00 g/ml x 100% = 25% error

7. Several answers apply. One possibility is to use a medicine dropper or a beral pipet to control dispensing the liquid in consistent volume amounts.

8. a) 120 g − 70 g = 50 g   b) 50 g / 50 ml = 1 g/ml

9. Oil is less dense than water and floats. It also does not mix with the polar solvent (H_2O) because it is nonpolar.

10. All mass measurements will be greater, so the density result (mass / volume) would be greater.

Lab: Density of Three Liquids   Name: _____

Purpose:
To measure the mass and volume of various liquid samples.
To graph the data and observe the relationship between the slope and density.

Materials:
Graduated cylinder   Balance
3 liquids provided by the teacher   Beaker or cup

Procedure:

1. Determine the mass of a clean, dry graduated cylinder.
2. Obtain approximately 30 mL of the liquid being measured in a small cup or beaker.
3. Add approximately 5 mL of the liquid to the graduated cylinder. Dry the outside if you have spilled any liquid. Record the volume of the liquid. Determine the mass of the cylinder with the liquid in it and record.
4. Add 5 mL more of the liquid to the cylinder, recording the mass and volume after each addition. Continue until you have completed 6 measurements.
5. Discard the liquid. Rinse and dry the beaker and the graduate cylinder between liquids. Measure three different liquids.

Laboratory Report Requirements
Label and skip a line between each section. Indicate if data tables and charts are attached on separate pages (ex. Data Table – see attached).

Title, Purpose, Materials, Procedure

Data
Density = mass / volume   Remember significant figure rules!

Sample Calculation
Show a sample calculation of density for one trial. Include identity of the sample, formula used, calculation and answer with units.
Collect and calculate the remaining results in the table provided.

Graph
Graph Mass vs. Volume (y vs. x) for all three sets of data on a single set of axes.
Plot the points for one liquid, and then draw a best-fit line that goes through the 0, 0 point. Complete one line before drawing the next data line.

Conclusion
In paragraph form, discuss the following ideas:

- For each of the three liquids, calculate the slope of the graph. Show your work.

- For each of the three liquids, calculate the average density based on the measurements. Show your work

- Compare the average density values of the three liquids to the slopes of the corresponding graphs. How close were the values?

- Describe how you would improve this lab using the same or similar materials.

Data: Liquid 1 - Water

Sample	Mass of water and cylinder (g)	Mass of dry cylinder (g)	Mass of Water (g)	Volume of Water (mL)	Density (g/mL)
1	-------------------	-------------------	0	0	-------------
2					
3					
4					
5					
6					
7					

Data: Liquid 2 – Alcohol

Sample	Mass of water and cylinder (g)	Mass of dry cylinder (g)	Mass of Water (g)	Volume of Water (mL)	Density (g/mL)
1	-------------------	-------------------	0	0	-------------
2					
3					
4					
5					
6					
7					

Data: Liquid 3 – Salt Water

Sample	Mass of water and cylinder (g)	Mass of dry cylinder (g)	Mass of Water (g)	Volume of Water (mL)	Density (g/mL)
1	-------------------	-------------------	0	0	-------------
2					
3					
4					
5					
6					
7					

Lab: Analysis of a Mixture

Summary
Student mixes measured samples of sand and salt. Water is mixed in, the mixture is filtered and the two substances dry overnight. The two dried substances are measured the next day and percent error is calculated for the amount of sand and salt recovered.

Student Skills:
Lab skill of physical separation using filtration
Calculation of percent error

Lab: Analysis of a Mixture — Teacher Information Page

Background:
This lab teaches basic lab skills and the students are required to evaluate their own laboratory results. Students experience the requirements of a working lab – a sample with a known composition is analyzed to test the lab's own process before applying it to unknown samples.

Many versions of this lab also add and separate iron filings. In my experience, separating iron filings is messy, time-consuming and doesn't add to what is being learned by the students. Sometimes the iron filings get wet and rust, increasing the mass of the results.

Also, many labs use a ring/ring-stand setup for the filtration process. I've accomplished this filtration with only a funnel and a beaker. The student props the funnel in the beaker or holds it up to prevent tipping over the whole system. Here, I opted to use less equipment.

This lab does not involve boiling water or a chemical reaction so plastic cups and spoons can be used.

> The teacher is expected to demonstrate the folding of the filter paper. As shown below, fold the filter paper in half, fold the filter paper in half again and peel back the outside layer of paper to make a cone.
>
>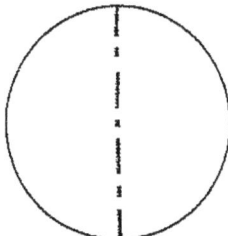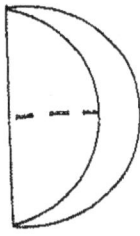
>
> The filtration process takes time, so decide if you want students to prepare their mixtures during one class session and then perform the separation during the next class session. In a hurry, students poke at the filter paper with their stirring rods in hopes of speeding up the filtration process. Usually the student pokes a hole in the filter paper, the mixture runs out and the entire lab must be started over.

I have included a step (#11) to rinse the filtrate by adding another 10 mL of water. This step may be eliminated if class time is limited.

Class Materials:

Sand	Salt	Filter paper	Beakers
Spoons	Balance	Water	Funnels
Watch-glasses	Labeling Markers		

Extra materials for the teacher:
Nothing!

Preparation:
Set up two stations, one with salt in a labeled container with a spoon and another labeled container with sand and a spoon.

During lab:
Monitor student progress and aid where appropriate.

Each student will have to label which beaker holds the sand and which holds the salt, #1 or #2.

> **Hint**
> To obtain sand, check with the Earth Science teacher at your school to see if there is any to spare (you may be in luck!) or check a local home improvement store – sand for sandboxes is available there. Salt is readily available at your local grocery store.

Pages to use for "Analysis of a Mixture":
10 question report: pages 33-34.
Full write-up: pages 36-37.

Possible ChemMatters article:
Brownlee, Christen, "The Quest for a Clean Drink", ChemMatters, April, 2008, pp.4-6, American Chemical Society.

This article describes how water contaminated with arsenic is filtered to make it safe to drink in India and Bangladesh.

This article is also a good supplement for the topics of **Oxidation and Reduction** and **Arsenic Poisoning**.

Directions of how to get the article online are on Page 2.

Sources:

http://webs.anokaramsey.edu/Chemistry/Chem1020/Labs/pdf/SandAndSalt.PDF

http://themalloryfamily.net/Physical_Science_Lab/Handouts/Lab%2012-Qualitative%20Separation%20of%20a%20Mixture.pdf

http://www.doccasagrande.net/Chem%201%20Files/Chem%201%20Chapter%2003%20Folder/Chem%201%20Chapter%2003%20Labs/LAB--Separation%20of%20a%20Mixture.pdf

Brownlee, Christen, "The Quest for a Clean Drink", ChemMatters, April, 2008, pp.4-6, American Chemical Society.

Lab: Analysis of a Mixture

Name _____

Purpose: To separate a sand-salt mixture and determine the percent error of sand and salt collected.

In working labs, samples with known compositions are analyzed to test the lab's own process before applying it to unknown samples.

Materials:
Sand	Salt	Filter paper	Markers
Beakers	Spoons	Balance	Water
Funnel	Watch glass		

Procedure:

Day One

1. Obtain two beakers. Label them with your initials, class section, and either #1 or #2.
2. Mass each beaker and record values.
3. Obtain and label a piece of filter paper. Mass and record.
4. Place one spoonful of sand in beaker #1. Mass and record.
5. Place one spoonful of salt in beaker #2. Mass and record.
6. Combine the sand and salt in one of the two beakers and mix with a spoon.
7. Add approximately 100 mL of water to the sand-salt mixture. Stir to dissolve the salt.
8. Fold and place the filter paper into funnel in the remaining empty beaker.
9. Carefully pour the sand-salt solution into the funnel.
   You may have to support the funnel by hand. Do not spill or allow any overflow.
   Filtering takes time -- poking the filter with your stirring rod won't speed things up!
10. Add approximately 20ml of water to the beaker to rinse out any sand left behind. Pour the mixture into the filter paper.
11. Once the mixture has drained, pour another 10 ml of water into the funnel and allow it to drain.
12. Carefully remove the filter paper and place on a watch glass. Place watch glass with filter paper/sand, and the beaker with salt water, where your teacher indicates.
13. Allow both to dry overnight.

Day Two

14. Mass dried filter paper with sand and record. Dispose of the sand and filter paper where your teacher indicates.
15. Mass the beaker with salt and record. Clean beaker with water.

Data Table

Before Separation:	
Mass Empty Beaker #1 (g)	
Mass Empty Beaker #2 (g)	
Initial Mass of Sand + Beaker #1 or 2	
Initial Mass of Salt + Beaker #1 or 2	
Mass Empty Filter Paper (g)	
After Separation:	
Mass Salt + Beaker #1 or 2	
Mass Filter Paper + Dry Sand (g)	

Questions

Answer these questions on your own paper. For questions #1-6, show all mathematical work including labeled answer with units. For questions #7-10, use full sentences (two sentences minimum).

1. Calculate the mass of sand before separation (accepted value).
2. Calculate the mass of sand after separation (measured value).
3. Calculate the percent error of sand collected.
4. Calculate the mass of salt before separation (accepted value).
5. Calculate the mass of salt after separation (measured value).
6. Calculate the percent error of salt collected.
7. Evaluate the quality of your results.
8. Describe one possible cause for the sand recovered being larger than what was originally used.
9. Describe one possible cause for the salt recovery being larger than what was originally used.
10. Describe how you would improve this lab using the same or similar materials.

Answer Key for "Analysis of a Mixture":

Sample data:

Before Separation:	
Mass Empty Beaker #1 (g)	100.00 g
Mass Empty Beaker #2 (g)	100.00 g
Initial Mass of Sand + Beaker #1	150.00 g
Initial Mass of Salt + Beaker #2	150.00 g
Mass Empty Filter Paper (g)	2.00 g
After Separation:	
Mass Salt + Beaker #1	148.00 g
Mass Filter Paper + Dry Sand (g)	53.00 g

1. (Mass of Sand + Beaker) – Mass of Beaker = Initial Mass of Sand
   150.00 g – 100.00 g = 50.00 g

2. (Mass of filter paper + Dry Sand) – Mass Empty Filter Paper = Final Mass of Sand
   53.00 g – 2.00 g = 51.00 g

3. % error = | measured value – accepted value | / accepted value x 100%
   % error sand = | 51.00 g – 50.00 g | / 50.00 g x 100% = 1.00 g / 50.00 g x 100% = 2.00% error

4. (Mass of Salt + Beaker) – Mass of Beaker = Initial Mass of Salt
   150.00 g – 100.00 g = 50.00 g

5. (Mass of Salt + Beaker) – Mass of Beaker = Final Mass of Salt
   148.00 g – 100.00 g = 48.00 g

6. % error = | measured value – accepted value | / accepted value x 100%
   % error salt = | 48.00 g – 50.00 g | / 50.00 g x 100%

   = 2.00 g / 50.00 g x 100% = 4.00% error

7. Several answers apply. Possibilities for poor results include that only one trial was completed, or that the procedure was rushed because the lab had to be started again due to poking a hole in the filter paper.

8. One possibility is that not all of the salt was washed out of the mixture, resulting in a sand value that was too big.

9. One possibility is that the salt was not completely dry, resulting in a salt value that was too big.

10. Several answers apply. One possibility is using a ring and ring stand to support the funnel during filtration.

Lab: Analysis of a Mixture   Name _____

Purpose: To separate a sand-salt mixture and determine the percent error of sand and salt collected.

In working labs, samples with known compositions are analyzed to test the lab's own process before applying it to unknown samples.

Materials:

Sand	Salt	Filter paper	Markers
Beakers	Spoons	Balance	Water
Funnel	Watch glass		

Procedure:

Day One

1. Obtain two beakers. Label them with your initials, class section, and either #1 or #2.
2. Mass each beaker and record values.
3. Obtain and label a piece of filter paper. Mass and record.
4. Place one spoonful of sand in beaker #1. Mass and record.
5. Place one spoonful of salt in beaker #2. Mass and record.
6. Combine the sand and salt in one of the two beakers and mix with a spoon.
7. Add approximately 100 mL of water to the sand-salt mixture. Stir to dissolve the salt.
8. Fold and place the filter paper into funnel in the remaining empty beaker.
9. Carefully pour the sand-salt solution into the funnel.
    You may have to support the funnel by hand. Do not spill or allow any overflow.
    Filtering takes time -- poking the filter with your stirring rod won't speed things up!
10. Add approximately 20ml of water to the beaker to rinse out any sand left behind. Pour the mixture into the filter paper.
11. Once the mixture has drained, pour another 10 ml of water into the funnel and allow it to drain.
12. Carefully remove the filter paper and place on a watch glass. Place watch glass with filter paper/sand, and the beaker with salt water, where your teacher indicates.
13. Allow both to dry overnight.

Day Two

14. Mass dried filter paper with sand and record. Dispose of the sand and filter paper where your teacher indicates.
15. Mass the beaker with salt and record. Clean beaker with water.

Data Table

Before Separation:	
Mass Empty Beaker #1 (g)	
Mass Empty Beaker #2 (g)	
Initial Mass of Sand + Beaker #1 or 2	
Initial Mass of Salt + Beaker #1 or 2	
Mass Empty Filter Paper (g)	
After Separation:	
Mass Salt + Beaker #1 or 2	
Mass Filter Paper + Dry Sand (g)	

Laboratory Report Requirements

Label and skip a line between each section. Label if data tables and charts are attached on separate pages (ex. Data Table – see attached)

Title, Purpose, Materials, Procedure

Data

Calculations -- Label and show mathematical work with units.

1. Mass of sand before separation (accepted value).
2. Mass of sand after separation (measured value).
3. Percent error of sand collected.
4. Mass of salt before separation (accepted value).
5. Mass of salt after separation (measured value).
6. Percent error of salt collected.

Conclusion

In paragraph form, discuss the following ideas:

- Evaluate the quality of your results.
- Describe one possible cause for the sand recovered being larger than what was originally used.
- Describe one possible cause for the salt recovery being larger than what was originally used.
- Describe how you would improve this lab using the same or similar materials.

Lab: Paper Chromatography

Summary
Student separates the components marker inks by performing paper chromatography. The test is performed with two solvents, a salt-water solution and an alcohol-water solution.

Student Skills:
Lab skill of physical separation using paper chromatography

Lab: Paper Chromatography — Teacher Information Page

Background:
The first time I performed this lab it used large sheets of chromatography paper and tall test tubes (about 15-20 cm tall). Many high school labs don't have either of these items, so I took the measurement and retention factor (R_f) aspects of the lab and combined it with materials easier to collect.

Most students have experienced this process as a fun activity, but now they can learn its useful applications. For example, gas chromatography could be researched by your students to show another version of this process.

Using pure water or pure alcohol for the solvents doesn't give very good separation results. 1% salt water and 10% alcohol water provides better results and use readily available chemicals. Directions for mixing are listed below.

> It's tempting to skip covering the system with plastic wrap; but, as the chromatography vessel (the cup) gets saturated with vapor, the progression of the liquid up the paper is slowed down and the separation results are much better.
> **Don't skip it!**

If you don't have filter paper in your laboratory, coffee filters from the local grocery store can be used. There are cone style (flat) filters (@ $2.50 for 100) that when split at the seam will provide enough paper for one trial. More common are rippled coffee filters (@ $1.50 for 200). The cone style are almost twice as expensive as rippled filters, but provide better separation results.

A cool iron can be used to press the rippled filters a little bit flatter. Best results are with ironing one to three filters at a time (versus ten at a time). This might be a way for a student to earn extra credit, and irons and boards may be available in the Consumer Sciences department of your school.

If lab time is limited, the filter paper can be cut out ahead of time. Patterns can be prepared out of card stock, manila folders or construction paper.

Some labs don't have many large beakers. Large, plastic cups available at the grocery store can be used (473 mL or 16 oz.). Clear plastic cups work well so that students can monitor the progress of the liquid as it moves up the paper.

Using markers from the same box yield results that are easy to compare. Your local dollar store is a good source for inexpensive markers.

Class Materials:
Filter paper or coffee filters
Pencils
Plastic wrap
Tall beakers (200 milliliter or larger)

Water soluble markers
Scissors
Rulers
Solvents

Extra materials for the teacher:
Nothing!

Preparation of Solutions:

1% NaCl solution:
Based on a mass percent solution, grams of solute per 100 grams of solution

(I assumed that the mass of solution is based on the density of water.)

1 g of sodium chloride in 100 g of solution is a 1 % by mass solution

For a larger volume (a 2 liter soda bottle, for example)

$$\frac{1 \text{ g NaCl}}{100 \text{ mL solution}} \times 2\,000 \text{ mL solution} = 20.00 \text{ g NaCl}$$

10% alcohol solution
Based on a volume percent solution, milliliters of solute per 100 mL of solution

10 mL of alcohol in 100 mL of solution

For a larger volume (a 2 liter soda bottle, for example)

$$\frac{10 \text{ mL alcohol}}{100 \text{ mL solution}} \times 2\,000 \text{ mL solution} = 200 \text{ mL alcohol}$$

For both solutions, add enough distilled water (solvent) to the salt or alcohol (solute) to mix the desired volume of solution.

During lab:
Monitor student progress and aid where appropriate.

Lab pages to use for "Paper Chromatography":
10 question report: pages 42-43 plus a data chart on page 44.
Full write-up: pages 46-47 plus a data chart on page 48.

To save photocopying, a blank data chart could be projected on the overhead or drawn on the blackboard for students to copy.

Possible ChemMatters article:

Shiber, Linda, "Sticky Situations: The Wonders of Glue", ChemMatters, December, 2006, pp. 8-10, American Chemical Society.

This article describes the attractive forces giving various glues their properties.

This article is also a good supplement for the topic of **Cross-Linked Polymers**.

Directions of how to get the article online are on Page 2.

Another option is a ChemMatters article on the CD ROM, but not online, is:
Miller, Steve, "King Midas: Leftovers From his Last Feast", ChemMatters, December, 2001, pp.4-5, American Chemical Society
This article describes how liquid and gas chromatography were used to analyze the 2700 year-old leftovers of a funeral feast for King Midas.

Sources:

Orna, Schreck and Heikkinen, Chemsource: Instructional Resources for Preservice and Inservice Chemistry Teachers, Volume 2, ChemSource, Inc., 1994. (Forensic Chemistry chapter, pp. 4-11)

http://www.byui.edu/chemistry/lab_manuals/chem_101/separations.pdf

http://scienceblogs.com/ethicsandscience/2007/07/fun_with_paper_chromatography.php

http://www.sirchie.com/Assets/Manuals/pdf/UPD/MZ020_TI02-45ENG-REV2E.pdf

http://abacus.bates.edu/~ganderso/biology/resources/dilutions.html

http://www.uwplatt.edu/chemep/chem/chemscape/labdocs/catofp/chromato/tlc/tlc.htm#chamber

http://www.docstoc.com/docs/22455616/THE-technique-of-chromatography-is-vastly-used-for-the/

Shiber, Linda, "Sticky Situations: The Wonders of Glue", ChemMatters, December, 2006, pp. 8-10, American Chemical Society.

Miller, Steve, "King Midas: Leftovers From his Last Feast", ChemMatters, December, 2001, pp.4-5, American Chemical Society.

Lab: Paper Chromatography   Name _____

Purpose: To learn the physical separation technique of paper chromatography and apply it to an unknown mixture.

Materials:

Filter paper   Water soluble markers
Pencils   Scissors
Plastic wrap   Rulers
Tall beakers or plastic cups (200 milliliter or larger)   Tape
1% salt solution   10% alcohol solution

Procedure:

Perform this procedure two times – each time with the same pen inks but changing the solvents.

Prepare the paper: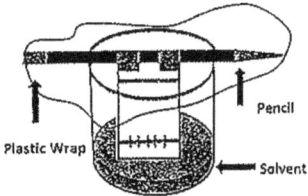

1. Cut out a piece of filter paper 14 cm tall x 6 cm wide and label the bottom right corner in pencil with your initials.

2. Draw two lines in pencil on your paper -- one 2 cm from the bottom of the paper and one 2 cm from the top of the paper. Measure along the bottom pencil line and draw 5 pencil marks 1 cm apart. You will spot your samples on the 5 marks.

3. Place dots of five different color inks on the 1 cm marks. Label the colors in pencil for later reference (R for red, G for green, etc.). Include a black ink sample.

4. Attach the top of the paper to the center of a pencil with tape. Put solvent in the cup to a depth of approximately 1/2 centimeter.

Chromatography:

5. Lay the pencil across the top of the cup so that the bottom edge of the paper strip barely touches the solvent. **The ink line should not be in the liquid.** Cover the beaker with the plastic wrap.

6. Allow the solvent to travel up the paper until it nears the top pencil line. Try not to let the solvent travel all the way to the top of the paper. Remove the pencil/paper setup from the cup.

7. Carefully cut the paper along the top line. Draw a pencil line along the top of the solvent to show how far the solvent traveled. Place it on a paper towel to dry.

8. After drying, measure the distance each color has moved from the bottom 2 cm line. If the ink separates into more than one color, measure the distance each component moved from the color's starting point. Measure vertically in a straight line, even if the ink color moved diagonally.

Data – attached.

Calculations

Retention Factor (R_f) = $\dfrac{\text{distance traveled by the sample component}}{\text{distance traveled by the solvent}}$

For example, $R_f = \dfrac{2.0 \text{ cm}}{5.0 \text{ cm}} = 0.40$

The R_f value has no units because the units of distance cancel.

Questions

Answer these questions on your own paper using full sentences -- either rewrite the question or incorporate it into your answer.

1. Explain why you mark the chromatography paper with pencil and not with pen.

2. Explain why the developing jar is covered with plastic wrap while performing paper chromatography.

3. Identify two physical properties that determine how well paper chromatography separates two different dyes in a mixture.

4. In 1% NaCl solution, which color moved the greatest distance? What does this indicate about this color?

5. In 1% NaCl solution, which color moved the least distance? What does this indicate about this color?

6. In 10% alcohol solution, which color moved the greatest distance? What does this indicate about this color?

7. In 10% alcohol solution, which color moved the least distance? What does this indicate about this color?

8. What were the components of the black ink color? Were other ink colors that were tested the components of this color? Support your conclusions with visual and R_f data.

9. Evaluate the quality of your results.

10. Describe how you would improve this lab using the same or similar materials.

Data:

1% NaCl solution

Solute Color	Solute Distance (cm)	Solvent Distance (cm)	Retention Factor (R_f)

10% isopropyl alcohol solution

Solute Color	Solute Distance (cm)	Solvent Distance (cm)	Retention Factor (R_f)

Answer Key for "Paper Chromatography":

1. Pencil is not water soluble and will not smear as the paper becomes wet.

2. The developing jar was covered while performing paper chromatography so that the atmosphere in the jar becomes saturated with solvent. This slows down the progress of the solvent up the paper and accomplishes a better separation of the colored components.

3. Solubility of the solute (ink) in the solvent is the major factor that accomplishes the separation of the components in the ink colors. Compounds which are not soluble in the solvent stay in place. Compounds that are very soluble travel up with the solvent.

   Another factor is the attraction of the solute to the chromatography paper (stationary phase) which causes the ink to move up the paper more slowly.

4. Answer dependent on sample data. Generally, colors that move the largest distance and have high R_f values are more soluble in the 1% NaCl solution.

5. Answer dependent on sample data. Generally, colors that move the least distance and have low R_f values are less soluble in the 1% NaCl solution.

6. Answer dependent on sample data. Generally, colors that move the largest distance and have high R_f values are more soluble in the 10% alcohol solution.

7. Answer dependent on sample data. Generally, colors that move the least distance and have low R_f values are less soluble in the 10% alcohol solution

8. Answer dependent on sample data.

9. Several answers apply. Possibilities include that results were limited because only one trial was completed in each solvent or that the chromatography paper was not completely flat (if a rippled coffee filter is used).

10. Several answers apply. Possibilities include completing multiple trials or ironing the filter paper to obtain a flatter sample.

Lab: Paper Chromatography   Name _____

Purpose: To learn the physical separation technique of paper chromatography and apply it to an unknown mixture.

Materials:
Filter paper
Pencils
Plastic wrap
Tall beakers or plastic cups (200 milliliter or larger)
1% salt solution

Water soluble markers
Scissors
Rulers
Tape
10% alcohol solution

Procedure:

Perform this procedure two times -- each time with the same pen inks but changing the solvents.

Prepare the paper:

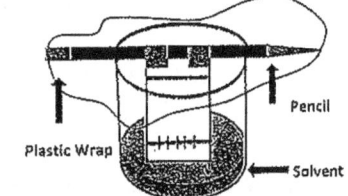

1. Cut out a piece of filter paper 14 cm tall x 6 cm wide and label the bottom right corner in pencil with your initials.

2. Draw two lines in pencil on your paper -- one 2 cm from the bottom of the paper and one 2 cm from the top of the paper. Measure along the bottom pencil line and draw 5 pencil marks 1 cm apart. You will spot your samples on the 5 marks.

3. Place dots of five different color inks on the 1 cm marks. Label the colors in pencil for later reference (R for red, G for green, etc.). Include a black ink sample.

4. Attach the top of the paper to the center of a pencil with tape. Put solvent in the cup to a depth of approximately 1/2 centimeter.

Chromatography:

5. Lay the pencil across the top of the cup so that the bottom edge of the paper strip barely touches the solvent. **The ink line should not be in the liquid.** Cover the beaker with the plastic wrap.

6. Allow the solvent to travel up the paper until it nears the top pencil line. Try not to let the solvent travel all the way to the top of the paper. Remove the pencil/paper setup from the cup.

7. Carefully cut the paper along the top line. Draw a pencil line along the top of the solvent to show how far the solvent traveled. Place it on a paper towel to dry.

8. After drying, measure the distance each color has moved from the bottom 2 cm line. If the ink separates into more than one color, measure the distance each component moved from the color's starting point. Measure vertically in a straight line, even if the ink color moved diagonally.

Data – attached.

Calculations

Retention Factor (R_f) = $\dfrac{\text{distance traveled by the sample component}}{\text{distance traveled by the solvent}}$

For example, $R_f = \dfrac{2.0 \text{ cm}}{5.0 \text{ cm}} = 0.40$

Notice that an R_f value has no units because the units of distance cancel.

Laboratory Report Requirements
Label and skip a line between each section. Label if data tables and charts are attached on separate pages (ex. Data Table – see attached).

Title

Purpose

Materials

Procedure

Data

Sample Calculation
Show a sample calculation of R_f for one trial. Include identity of the sample, formula used, calculation and answer with units.
Collect and calculate the remaining results in the Data Table.

Conclusion
In paragraph form, discuss the following ideas:

- In 1% NaCl solution, which color moved the greatest distance? The least distance? What does this indicate about each of these colors?

- In 10% alcohol solution, which color moved the greatest distance? The least distance? What does this indicate about each of these colors?

- Evaluate the quality of your results.

- Describe how you would improve this lab using the same or similar materials.

Data:

1% NaCl solution

Solute Color	Solute Distance (cm)	Solvent Distance (cm)	Retention Factor (R_f)

10% isopropyl alcohol solution

Solute Color	Solute Distance (cm)	Solvent Distance (cm)	Retention Factor (R_f)

Lab: Catching Moles

Summary
Student masses 100 dried beans of one type. This is repeated for three different types of bean. A relative mass scale is calculated based on the smallest bean. Student then masses a relative mass of each type of bean and counts the number of beans. The relative mass contains approximately the same number of beans for each type.

Students may work in groups of two.

Student Skills:
To develop the concept of relative mass

Lab: Catching Moles   **Teacher Information Page**

Background:

The concepts of *relative mass* and *the mole* are rather abstract and are difficult for students to grasp. This lab is a simulation of using relative mass to count atoms. This is done using objects that can be manipulated (dried beans) and calculating the relative mass.

I remember a student of mine was very frustrated early in the school year. He said, "Ms. Heesemann, I just don't get this mole thing." My response was, "You might not understand it right away, but keep using it, and it will eventually make sense." Months later, he said to me, "You were right! I get it now!"

Class Materials:
Samples of dried beans   200 ml beakers or other weighing containers
Balance   calculator

Materials for the teacher:
Nothing!

Preparation:
Collect the dried beans. Obtain airtight containers to store the beans for class use. Use the containers to store the beans for later years.

I found variations of this lab that use hard candies instead of beans. I opted not to tempt the students to eat in the chemistry laboratory and used the dried beans.

The math is simple, but you may want to go through the calculations as a class (Steps 3, 4 & 5) after the data in Step 1 is collected.

A series of sample calculations for Steps 3, 4 & 5 with sample data follow.

Step 3.   Average mass of bean #1:   25 g / 100 beans   = 0.25 g / bean #1

               Average mass of bean #2:   500 g / 100 beans   = 5 g / bean #2

Step 4.   Relative Mass = $\dfrac{\text{Average mass of one bean}}{\text{Average mass of the lightest bean tested}}$

               Relative Mass of Bean #1:   0.25 g / 0.25 g = 1

               Relative Mass of Bean #2:   5 g / 0.25 g = 20

               The masses have a ratio of 1 : 20.

               The Relative Mass now has the unit of grams added for easier use in lab.

Step 5: Number of beans in one relative mass = $\dfrac{\text{Relative mass}}{\text{Average mass of one bean}}$

Number of bean #1 in one relative mass: 1 g / 0.25 g/bean = 4 beans in 1 relative mass

Number of bean #2 in one relative mass: 20 g / 5 g/bean = 4 beans in 1 relative mass

There is some room on the bottom of the data page for students to follow along with the class calculations. Your students will appreciate the guidance.

The students then prove the relative mass relationship in Step 6 of the lab.

You may want to complete the atomic mass chart in the Conclusions section as a class as well.

Pages to use for "Catching Moles
10 question report: pages 52-53.
Full write-up: pages 55-56.

Possible ChemMatters article:
Ruth, Carolyn, "Where Do Chemical Elements Come From?", ChemMatters, October, 2009, pp.6-8, American Chemical Society.

This article describes the formation of elements and compounds during a supernova explosion of a star. This article is also a good supplement for the topics of **The Periodic Table, Nuclear Chemistry** and **Spectroscopy.**

Directions of how to get the article online are on Page 2.

Sources:
Orna, Schreck and Heikkinen, Chemsource: Instructional Resources for Preservice and Inservice Chemistry Teachers, Volume 2, ChemSource, Inc., 1994. (The Mole chapter, pp. 4-7)

http://www.chemistryexplained.com/Ma-Na/Mole-Concept.html

http://www.nwr1biology.com/pdfs/C4L_The_Mole-Bean_Lab.pdf

http://www.lapeer.org/chemcom/Unit2/2C.3MoleLabActivity.html

http://mr-paullers-wiki.wikispaces.com/file/view/Exp13BeanLab.pdf

http://faculty.oprfhs.org/lremack/SM2%20Chemistry/Quarter%203/Chapter%2010/Understanding%20the%20Mole.pdf

Ruth, Carolyn, "Where Do Chemical Elements Come From?", ChemMatters, October, 2009, pp.6-8, American Chemical Society.

Lab: Catching Moles   Name _____

Purpose:
This lab is a simulation of using relative mass to count atoms. This is done using objects that can be handled (dried beans) and calculating their relative mass.

Background:
It can be easier to count small objects in groups of 10 or 12 rather than counting them one by one. For example, eggs and donuts are sold by the dozen.

In chemistry, we count small particles (atoms or molecules) in groups called *moles*. The word is short for the German word "molekulargewicht" which means "molecular weight."

This experiment is completed using different kinds of dried beans, something easier to count in lab, to help you understand this system.

Materials
Samples of dried beans   150 mL beakers or weighing containers
Balance   calculator

Procedure

1. Measure the mass of an empty 150 mL beaker and record.

2. Add 100 whole beans of a particular type to the beaker and mass. Subtract the mass of the empty container to obtain the mass of the beans alone.

Complete Steps 1 & 2 for three different types of bean.

3. Using your data, calculate the *average mass* of one of each type of bean.

    Average mass of one bean = Mass of 100 beans / 100 beans = # grams / one bean

4. Determine the *relative mass* for each type of bean:

    Relative Mass = $\dfrac{\text{Average mass of one bean}}{\text{Average mass of the lightest bean tested}}$

5. Using your data, calculate the *number of beans in one relative mass* for each type of bean.

    Number of beans in one relative mass = $\dfrac{\text{Relative mass}}{\text{Average mass of one bean}}$

6. Check the accuracy of your relative masses for all three types of beans:
    a. Place your beaker on the balance and set it to zero.
    b. Add beans until the balance reads the values of one relative mass of that type bean (or as close as possible).
    c. Count the beans and record the number of beans in one relative mass.

Lab Data:

Type of bean			
Mass of 100 beans (g)			
*Average mass of 1 bean (g)			
*Relative mass			
*Predicted number of beans in one relative mass			
Measured number of beans in one relative mass			

*Calculated value.

Questions

Answer questions #1-5 on your own paper using full sentences -- either rewrite the question or incorporate it into your answer. This page with a completed chart below may be turned in for questions #6-10.

1. What did you find out about the number of beans in one relative mass? How do your calculated values compare to your measured values?

2. Evaluate the quality of your results.

3. Describe how you would improve this lab using the same materials.

4. How many atoms of a pure element are in one relative mass?

5. What is the name given to the number of atoms in a relative mass?

For questions #6-10, complete the chart below listing different elements.
    a. Mass relative to hydrogen = Mass of one atom / Mass of one atom of hydrogen
    b. Look up the atomic mass of each element on the periodic table
    c. Number of atoms in one relative mass = Relative mass / Average mass of one atom

Atom	6. H	7. C	8. Al	9. Cu	10. Pb
Mass of 1 atom	1.66×10^{-24}	2.00×10^{-23}	4.49×10^{-23}	1.05×10^{-22}	3.44×10^{-22}
Mass relative to hydrogen					
Atomic mass on periodic table					
Number of atoms in a relative mass					

Answer Key for "Catching Moles":

1. There were approximately the same number of beans in a relative mass. The measured values may be slightly under/over the number in a relative mass because the beans cannot be cut into smaller pieces.

2. Answers vary based on lab results. One possibility is that the measured number of beans was slightly under/over because the beans cannot be cut into smaller pieces.

3. Answers vary based on lab results. One possibility is to try different types of beans, with different masses per bean, and see if the concept still applies,

4. 6.023×10^{23} atoms are in a relative mass.

5. The number of atoms in a relative mass is Avogadro's number and is named after Amadeo Avogadro.

Atom	6. H	7. C	8. Al	9. Cu	10. Pb
Mass of 1 atom	1.66×10^{-24}	2.00×10^{-23}	4.49×10^{-23}	1.05×10^{-22}	3.44×10^{-22}
Mass relative to hydrogen	1	12.05	27.05	63.25	207.2
Atomic mass on periodic table	1.01	12.01	26.98	63.55	207.2
Number of atoms in a relative mass	6.02×10^{23}	6.02×10^{23}	6.02×10^{23}	6.02×10^{23}	6.02×10^{23}

Relative Mass =   Mass of one atom
(to hydrogen)   Mass of the lightest atom tested (hydrogen)

For carbon: 2.00×10^{-23} g / 1.66×10^{-24} g = 12.05

Number of atoms in one relative mass =   Mass relative to hydrogen
                                                        Average mass of one bean

For carbon: 12.05 g / 2.00×10^{-23} g/atom = 6.02×10^{23} atoms

Lab: Catching Moles   Name _____

Purpose:
This lab is a simulation of using relative mass to count atoms. This is done using objects that can be handled (dried beans) and calculating their relative mass.

Background:
It can be easier to count small objects in groups of 10 or 12 rather than counting them one by one. For example, eggs and donuts are sold by the dozen.

In chemistry, we count small particles (atoms or molecules) in groups called *moles*. The word is short for the German word "molekulargewicht" which means "molecular weight."

This experiment is completed using different kinds of dried beans, something easier to count in lab, to help you understand this system.

Materials
Samples of dried beans   150 mL beakers or weighing containers
Balance   calculator

Procedure

1. Measure the mass of an empty 150 mL beaker and record.

2. Add 100 whole beans of a particular type to the beaker and mass. Subtract the mass of the empty container to obtain the mass of the beans alone.

Complete Steps 1 & 2 for three different types of bean.

3. Using your data, calculate the *average mass* of one bean of each type:

   Average mass of one bean = Mass of 100 beans / 100 beans = # grams / one bean

4. Determine the *relative mass* for each type of bean:

   Relative Mass = $\dfrac{\text{Average mass of one bean}}{\text{Average mass of the lightest bean tested}}$

5. Using your data, calculate the *number of beans in one relative mass* for each type of bean.

   Number of beans in one relative mass = $\dfrac{\text{Relative mass}}{\text{Average mass of one bean}}$

6. Check the accuracy of your relative masses for all three types of beans:

   a. Place your beaker on the balance and set it to zero.
   b. Add beans until the balance reads the values of one relative mass of that type bean (or as close as possible).
   c. Count the beans and record the number of beans in one relative mass.

Lab Data:

Type of bean				
Mass of 100 beans (g)				
*Average mass of 1 bean (g)				
*Relative mass				
*Predicted number of beans in one relative mass				
Measured number of beans in one relative mass				

*Calculated value.

Laboratory Report Requirements
Label and skip a line between each section. Data tables and charts attached on separate pages are to be labeled (ex. Data Table – see attached).

Title, Purpose, Materials, Procedure
Data This page may be attached to the lab.

Conclusion
In paragraph form, discuss the following ideas, and attach the completed chart below.

- What did you find out about the number of beans in one relative mass? How do your calculated values compare to your measured values?
- What is the name given to the number of atoms in a relative mass?
- Evaluate the quality of your results.

Complete the chart below which lists different elements.
  a. Mass relative to hydrogen = Mass of one atom / Mass of one atom of hydrogen
  b. Look up the atomic mass of each element on the periodic table
  c. Number of atoms in one relative mass = Relative mass / Average mass of one atom

Atom	H	C	Al	Cu	Pb
Mass of 1 atom	1.66×10^{-24}	2.00×10^{-23}	4.49×10^{-23}	1.05×10^{-22}	3.44×10^{-22}
Mass relative to hydrogen					
Atomic mass on periodic table					
Number of atoms in a relative mass					

Lab: Moles in Your Name?

Summary
Student masses a piece of chalk before and after writing with it and calculates the mass, moles, formula units and atoms of chalk (calcium carbonate) used.

Student Skills:
Mathematical conversion of mass to moles
Mathematical conversion of moles to particles (molecules, formula units, atoms)
Significant figures in measurements and calculations

Lab: Moles in Your Name?   **Teacher Information Page**

Background:
This lab was the result of the need for a quick activity to make the mole concept less abstract to students. Your class will enjoy seeing the chalkboard covered with their names.

Chalkboards are being phased out with many school renovations, so finding boards and chalk in stores is difficult. I found chalk in the art department of an office supply store. Try online, and don't give up!

Some options for obtaining blackboards include the following.

- Use "sidewalk chalk" and have your students write on the pavement outside the school. If you do this, clarify with your school the procedures for moving your class to an alternate location.

- Purchase small, individual chalkboards at a local store.

- Make chalkboards using chalkboard paint (available for to brush on or to spray paint) by painting poster board or corrugated cardboard. Paint with two coats to get a better chalkboard surface. You could even offer extra credit to students to come in after school and make chalkboards for class use!

- Get a technology class to make portable chalkboards.

This is a brief lab, only a one-page handout for either a 10-question or full write-up format.

Class Materials:
Chalk   Balance   Chalkboard   Calculator

Materials for the teacher:
Nothing!

Preparation:
Set up a balance and erase the chalkboard.

During lab:
Circulate to observe and aid students working.

Pages to use for "Moles in Your Name?":
10 question report: page 60.
Full write-up: page 62.

Possible ChemMatters article:
Michalovic, Mark, "The Race for Iodine", ChemMatters, December, 2006, pp.18-19, American Chemical Society.

This article describes the history of the discovery of the element iodine. This article is also a good supplement for the topic of the **Periodic Table**.

Directions of how to get the article online are on Page 2.

Sources:

Dorin, Henry, <u>Chemistry: The Study of Matter</u>, Needham, MA, Prentice Hall, Inc., 1992.

Wilbraham, Antony C., et al., <u>Chemistry</u>, Menlo Park, CA, Prentice Hall, 2000.

http://misterguch.brinkster.net/oct2003.pdf

http://en.wikipedia.org/wiki/Gold_bar

Michalovic, Mark, "The Race for Iodine", ChemMatters, December, 2006, pp.18-19, American Chemical Society.

Lab: Moles in Your Name?   Name _____

Purpose:
To use the molar mass of calcium carbonate to determine the moles/particles/atoms in various masses of chalk.

Materials:
Balance   Chalk   Chalkboard   Calculator

Procedure:
1. Mass chalk and record.
2. Use the chalk to write your first and last name.
3. Mass chalk again and record.
4. Use the chalk to write the phrase, "CHEMISTRY RULES!".
5. Mass chalk a third time and record.

Data

Mass before writing name (g)	
Mass after writing name (g)	
Mass of name (g)	
Mass before writing phrase (g)	
Mass after writing phrase (g)	
Mass of phrase (g)	

Questions
Answer these questions on your own paper -- either rewrite the question or incorporate it into the answer. Show any mathematical work including units.

1. How many moles of calcium carbonate ($CaCO_3$) were in the original piece of chalk?
2. What mass of calcium carbonate was used to write your name?
3. How many moles of calcium carbonate were used to write your name?
4. How many formula units of calcium carbonate were used to write your name?
5. How many atoms were used to write your name?
6. What mass of calcium carbonate was used to write "CHEMISTRY RULES"?
7. How many moles of calcium carbonate were used to write "CHEMISTRY RULES"?
8. How many formula units of calcium carbonate were used to write "CHEMISTRY RULES"?
9. How many atoms were used to write "CHEMISTRY RULES"?
10. The standard gold bar held by central banks is 12.4 kg. How many moles of gold are in one bar? How many atoms of gold are in one bar? Show your work with units.

Answer Key for "Moles in Your Name?"

Sample data is used for questions #1 - #9:

1. 20 g chalk → gram formula mass of $CaCO_3$ = 40 + 12 + 3(16) = 100 →

    20 g x 1 mole/100 g = 0.2 mol $CaCO_3$

2. 20 g – 15 g = 5 g

3. 5 g x 1 mole/100 g = 0.05 mol $CaCO_3$

4. 0.05 mol x 6.023 x 10^{23} formula units / mole = 3.01 x 10^{22} formula units

    $CaCO_3$ is an ionic compound. Referring to $CaCO_3$ as being composed of molecules is not correct and should use the term *formula units* to describe the building blocks.

5. 3.01 x 10^{22} formula units x 5 atoms / formula unit = 1.51 x 10^{23} atoms

6. 15 – 8 g = 7 g

7. 7 g x 1 mole/100 g = 0.07 mol $CaCO_3$

8. 0.07 mol x 6.023 x 10^{23} formula units / mole = 4.22 x 10^{22} formula units

9. 4.22 x 10^{22} formula units x 5 atoms / formula unit = 2.11 x 10^{23} atoms

10. 12.4 kg x 1000 g/1kg = 12 400 g

    12 400 g x 1 mole Au/ 196.97 g = 62.95 mole Au

    62.95 mole Au x 6.023 x 10^{23} atoms/1 mole = 3.29 x 10^{25} atoms Au

Lab: Moles in Your Name?   Name _____

Purpose:
To use the molar mass of calcium carbonate to determine the moles/particles/atoms in various masses of chalk.

Materials:
Balance   Chalk   Chalkboard   Calculator

Procedure:
1. Mass chalk and record.
2. Use the chalk to write your first and last name.
3. Mass chalk again and record.
4. Use the chalk to write the phrase, "CHEMISTRY RULES!".
5. Mass chalk a third time and record.

Data

Mass before writing name (g)	
Mass after writing name (g)	
Mass of name (g)	
Mass before writing phrase (g)	
Mass after writing phrase (g)	
Mass of phrase (g)	

Laboratory Report Requirements
Label and skip a line between each section.

Title, Purpose, Materials, Procedure, Data

Calculations -- For all calculations, label and show the work with units.
1) Calculate the mass, moles, formula units and atoms used to write your name.
2) Calculate the mass, moles, formula units and atoms used to write "CHEMISTRY RULES".

Conclusion
In paragraph form, discuss the following ideas:
- Evaluate the quality of your results.
- Describe how you would improve this lab using the same or similar materials.
- Describe the lab steps to measure a glass of water to determine the mass/ moles/ atoms in the sample.
- The standard gold bar held by central banks is 12.4 kg. How many moles of gold are in one bar? How many atoms of gold are in one bar? Show your work with units.

Lab: A Chemical Reaction

Summary
Student measures a mass of sodium bicarbonate and adds hydrochloric acid to produce the following reaction:

$$HCl\ (aq) + NaHCO_3\ (aq) \longrightarrow NaCl\ (aq) + H_2CO_3\ (aq) \longrightarrow NaCl\ (aq) + H_2O\ (l) + CO_2\ (g)$$

The carbon dioxide gas bubbles away and the water and excess hydrochloric acid evaporate out of the system.

The dried sodium chloride product is massed and percent yield is calculated based on a calculated theoretical yield.

Student Skills:
Stoichiometry
Significant figures (measurement and calculation)
Calculation of percent yield

Lab: A Chemical Reaction   **Teacher Information Page**

Background:
This is a simple chemical reaction that produces very good results.

Many labs in my research instruct to heat the mixture over a Bunsen burner with a ring stand/ring/wire gauze setup, or with a hot-plate or a drying oven. In all of these situations, I have experienced *bumping.* The water has boiled away so much that the water vapor gets trapped under the very concentrated solution. This results in the *bump* sound when it escapes. It can spray some of the concentrated salt solution out of the beaker and reducing the percent yield.

I have had very good results, almost 100% yield, by simply letting the mixture evaporate. It takes about two days, but it's worth it because the results are great!

Beral Pipettes make adding just enough HCl easier. If they're not available, the acid could be poured from a small beaker (50 mL for example).

Solid, plastic stirring rods (like those used for drinks) can be used if glass stirring rods are not available. **Solid** stirring rods are recommended, not the hollow stirrers typically provided for coffee.

For a full lab-write-up, a teacher may choose to have students attach the completed lab sheet for their Data.

Laboratory Safety:
Students must wear laboratory safety goggles while performing this lab. The concentration of the HCl is low, but a gas is being produced so bubbles and possible splattering can happen.

It's always best to err on the side of caution when it comes to student safety! Also, remind students to wash their hands after the lab so they do not accidentally rub acid in their eyes!

---

*Note for parents who home school:
Some parents who home school and are interested in the labs in this book and I think they are useful. For your safety, **DO NOT PERFORM THIS LAB, INCLUDING THE DILUTION OF THE MURIATIC ACID, UNLESS YOU ARE A STATE BOARD CERTIFIED CHEMISTRY TEACHER OR HAVE A COLLEGE DEGREE IN CHEMISTRY, AND BOTH YOU AND THE STUDENT(S) ARE WEARING LABORATORY SAFETY GOGGLES DURING THE PERFORMANCE OF THIS LAB AND THE DILUTION OF THE ACID.**

Class Materials:
Beakers or plastic cups
Baking soda ($NaHCO_3$)
Non-water soluble markers
Scoopula or plastic spoons
 (to dispense baking soda)
3M HCl

Materials for the teacher:
Graduated cylinder (1 Liter)
Container for dispensing HCl during lab (2 Liter plastic soda bottle works well)

Preparation:
Dilute the hydrochloric acid according to what is available.

Safety is important when diluting an acid. The acid dilution is exothermic and heats up, so you add the acid to the water to dissipate the heat produced. If you add the water to the acid, the water could heat up and splash out of the mixing container.

An old saying in the laboratory is:

"Do what you oughta, add acid to watah!"

*ALWAYS mix volatile liquids with another adult able to aid if you call for help.** If there is an accident, you want to be able to contact someone easily. Some schools have phones in the rooms, but if you need help you might not be able to get to a phone. Make sure they're close enough to hear you!

Even though it's tempting to work at a time that's convenient to you, **WHEN YOU WORK WITH VOLATILE CHEMICALS, ALWAYS HAVE ANOTHER ADULT AVAILABLE TO HELP IN CASE OF AN ACCIDENT.**

What if your lab doesn't have any hydrochloric acid?
If you need to prepare 3M hydrochloric acid for this lab, *muriatic acid* bought at a local hardware store can be used.

Muriatic acid is 8-10 M hydrochloric acid used for swimming pool maintenance, to clean brick and metal, and to etch concrete. Muriatic acid is the older name for HCl that was replaced later with hydrochloric acid, a name in the IUPAC system (International Union of Practical and Applied Chemistry).

Muriatic acid is sold in a range of concentrations from 32-38% and prices range from $3.59 to $15.00 per gallon. It can be obtained at hardware stores or home improvement stores.

How much muriatic acid should you use?
Here's a method to figure out how much muriatic acid to use for 3M hydrochloric acid:

1. The percentage of muriatic acid x 10 **is approximately** the number of grams of HCl in 1000 mL of solution.

2. Convert the grams of HCl into moles of HCl by dividing by its molar mass (36 g/mole). This calculates the approximate moles per liter of HCl, or the approximate molarity of the concentrated HCl (muriatic acid).

3. Using the formula for dilution, you can determine the volume of the concentrated muriatic acid to use:

$$\text{molarity}_{concentrated} \times \text{volume}_{concentrated} = \text{molarity}_{diluted} \times \text{volume}_{diluted}$$

$$M_{concentrated} \times X \text{ mL} = 3.0 \text{ M} \times 1000 \text{ mL}$$

$$X \text{ mL}_{concentrated} = 3000 / M_{concentrated}$$

For example:
The bottle label reads 31.45% muriatic acid by weight

31.45 x 10 = 314.5 g HCl in 1000 mL concentrated acid or 314.5 g/L

$$\frac{314.5 \text{ g HCl}}{1 \text{ L}} \times \frac{1 \text{ mol HCl}}{36 \text{ g HCl}} = @ 8.7 \text{ mol/liter or } 8.7 \text{ Molar HCl}$$

$$\frac{8.7 \text{ M} \times \text{Volume}_{concentrated}}{8.7 \text{ M}} = \frac{3.0 \text{ M} \times 1000 \text{ mL}}{8.7 \text{ M}} = 345 \text{ mL of the concentrated HCl}$$

345 mL of 31.45% muriatic acid mixed with water to make 1000 mL of approximately 3.0 M hydrochloric acid

Remember to wear eye safety goggles while mixing this solution! Wear a rubberized lab apron to protect from acid spills!

To mix safely and dissipate the heat released, pour half of the water into the main container being used. Add half of the acid being used. Stopper. Mix (easily accomplished by simply inverting the **stoppered** container). Add another quarter of the water being used. Add the rest of the acid. Stopper and mix. Finally, add enough water to make 1000 mL of 3 molar HCl solution.

*Fortunately, the HCl is used in excess for this lab, so the exact concentration is not important to the accuracy of the result.

During lab:
Enforce student safety and wearing of eye safety goggles.

Remind students:

    (a) where to place labeled containers to dry overnight;

    (b) to wash their remaining lab glassware;

    (c) where to dispose of lab waste;

    (d) to wash their hands with soap and water.

Pages to use for "A Chemical Reaction":
10 question report: pages 68-69.
Full write-up: pages 71-72.

Possible ChemMatters article:
Husband, Tom, "Recycling Aluminum: A Way of Life or a Lifestyle?" ChemMatters, April, 2012, pp. 15-17, American Chemical Society.

This article describes the chemical reactions involved in recycling aluminum.

This article also discusses the **Electrochemistry** in the conversion of aluminum oxide to pure aluminum metal.

Directions of how to get the article online are on Page 2.

Another possibility is:
Kimbrough, Doris R., "Chemistry Goes Underground", ChemMatters, April, 2002, pp.7-9, American Chemical Society.
This article describes the slow chemical reactions that form caverns.

Sources:
http://www.smglabbooks.com/downloads/Sample_Experiment_6B_v02.pdf

http://www.teacherweb.com/CA/CastroValleyHighSchool/Yager/VinegarBakingSodaStoichiometryLab.pdf

http://www.naturalhandyman.com/iip/infxtra/infmur.html

http://serendip.brynmawr.edu/sci_edu/farber/wheretopurchase.html

Husband, Tom, "Recycling Aluminum: A Way of Life or a Lifestyle?" ChemMatters, April, 2012, pp. 15-17, American Chemical Society.

Kimbrough, Doris R., "Chemistry Goes Underground", ChemMatters, April, 2002, pp.7-9, American Chemical Society.

Lab: A Chemical Reaction   Name _____

Purpose: To perform a decomposition reaction, measure the reactants and products, and calculate the percent yield of the reaction.

Materials:
Beakers or plastic cups
Baking soda (NaHCO₃)
Beral pipette

Scoopula or plastic spoons
 (to dispense baking soda)
3M HCl
Stirring rod

SAFETY: Wearing lab safety goggles is required during this lab. Wash your hands after cleaning up.

Procedure:
1. Label a clean, dry beaker (150 mL or larger) and mass.
2. Add about one-scoopula of baking soda (NaHCO₃) to the beaker and mass.
3. Obtain 5-7 ml of 3M HCl in a 2nd beaker.
4. Add the hydrochloric acid to the baking soda in small portions, mixing with a stirring rod after each addition.
5. Continue adding acid <u>until</u> the reaction stops producing bubbles.
6. Place the container to dry where your teacher indicates.
7. Mass the dried container with salt produced.
8. Clean the container.

Data

Mass of empty beaker (g)	
Mass of beaker with NaHCO₃ (g)	
Mass of beaker with NaCl (g)	

Questions

Answer these questions on your own paper using full sentences -- either rewrite the question or incorporate it into the answer.

1. Write a balanced chemical reaction for the reaction that occurred between the hydrochloric acid and the sodium bicarbonate including phases.
2. Calculate the mass of sodium bicarbonate.
3. Calculate the moles of sodium bicarbonate.
4. Based on balanced chemical reaction, calculate the moles of sodium chloride that should be produced (theoretical yield).
5. Calculate the mass of sodium chloride that should be produced (theoretical yield).
6. Calculate the mass of sodium chloride produced in this lab (actual yield).
7. Calculate the percent error of sodium chloride produced.
8. Calculate the percent yield of your lab value of NaCl. What is the best percent yield value possible?
9. Explain why you stopped adding hydrochloric acid when the bubbling stopped.
10. Describe how you would improve this lab using the same or similar materials. If your results were very good, explain what was important to obtaining those good results.

Answer Key for "A Chemical Reaction":

1. HCl (aq) + NaHCO$_3$ (s) --> NaCl (aq) + H$_2$O (l) + CO$_2$ (g)

Sample data is used for questions #2 - #8:

2. 125 g – 100 g = 25 g

3. gram formula mass = 23 + 1 + 12 + 3(16) = 84

    25 g x 1 mole/84 g = 0.30 moles NaHCO$_3$

4. 0.30 mol NaHCO$_3$ x 1 mol NaCl / 1 mol NaHCO$_3$ = 0.30 mol NaCl

5. 0.30 mol NaCl x 58 g / mol = 17.4 g NaCl

6. 117 g – 100 g = 17 g

7. $$\frac{|17.4 \text{ g} - 17 \text{ g}|}{17.4 \text{ g}} \times 100\% = 2.3\% \text{ error}$$

    The best percent error value possible is 0% error.

8. 17 g / 17.4 g x   100 % = 97.7 % yield

    The best percent yield value possible is 100%.

9. This lab produces very good results. One reason for success is careful adding of the acid so that the reaction does not bubble out of the beaker.

10. The bubbling stops when there isn't any more sodium bicarbonate (NaHCO$_3$) left to react to produce carbon dioxide (CO$_2$) which indicates that the reaction is complete.

Lab: A Chemical Reaction   Name _____

Purpose: To perform a decomposition reaction, measure the reactants and products, and calculate the percent yield of the reaction.

Materials:
Beakers or plastic cups
Baking soda ($NaHCO_3$)
Beral pipette

Scoopula or plastic spoons
 (to dispense baking soda)
3M HCl
Stirring rod

SAFETY: Wearing lab safety goggles is required during this lab. Wash your hands after cleaning up.

Procedure:
1. Label a clean, dry beaker (150 mL or larger) and mass.
2. Add about one-scoopula of baking soda ($NaHCO_3$) to the beaker and mass.
3. Obtain 5-7 ml of 3M HCl in a 2nd beaker.
4. Add the hydrochloric acid to the baking soda in small portions, mixing with a stirring rod after each addition.
5. Continue adding acid <u>until</u> the reaction stops producing bubbles.
6. Place the container to dry where your teacher indicates.
7. Mass the dried container with salt produced.
8. Clean the container.

Data

Mass of empty beaker (g)	
Mass of beaker with $NaHCO_3$ (g)	
Mass of beaker with NaCl (g)	

Laboratory Report Requirements

Label and skip a line between each section.
Data tables and charts attached on separate pages are to be labeled (ex. Data Table – see attached).

Title, Purpose, Materials, Procedure

Data

Calculations
Label each calculation and show all work with units.

1. Calculate the mass and moles of sodium bicarbonate used in the reaction.
2. Based on balanced chemical reaction, calculate the moles of sodium chloride that should be produced (theoretical yield).
3. Calculate the mass of sodium chloride that should be produced (theoretical yield).
4. Calculate the mass of sodium chloride produced in this lab (actual yield).
5. Calculate the percent error of sodium chloride produced.
6. Calculate the percent yield of your lab value of NaCl. What is the best percent yield value possible?

Conclusion
In paragraph form, discuss the following ideas:

- Write a balanced chemical reaction for the reaction that occurred between the hydrochloric acid and the sodium bicarbonate including phases.

- Explain why you stopped adding hydrochloric acid when the bubbling stopped.

- What is the best percent error value possible? Based on your percent error value, evaluate the quality of your results.

- Describe how you would improve this lab using the same or similar materials. If your results were very good, explain what was important to obtaining those good results.

Lab: Molar Volume

Summary:
Student collects butane gas from a lighter by water displacement. The volume of the gas is measured. The atmospheric pressure, water temperature and mass difference of the lighter are recorded. The volume of the gas under standard conditions (STP), the molar volume (liter/mole), and the percent error are calculated.

Student Skills:
Mole conversions
Calculations using the combined gas law (PV/T = PV/T)

Lab: Molar Volume   **Teacher Information Page**

Background:

This is an easy way to collect a gas sample and perform the measurements necessary to determine molar volume.

A graduated cylinder can be used to collect the butane (C_4H_{10}), but it can be narrow and difficult to use. Here I have used plastic baby bottles to collect the gas. They are available at a dollar store or a grocery store. The volume markings may not be as accurate as the graduated cylinder so water from the baby bottle is measured with a graduated cylinder to verify the amount of gas collected.

Be sure to submerge lighters in water for 30 seconds and dry before the initial massing because water can get into the lighter and increase the mass.

A student would probably work better with a partner so that one student could hold the baby bottle while the other student holds the lighter and releases the butane gas under water.

The data table has room for two data trials. If there are time or material constraints, the teacher can choose to have one student pair share data with another student pair.

Some classrooms have barometers and atmospheric pressure can be measured immediately; however, if that is not available, the Internet can be used to obtain local atmospheric pressure data.

At http://www.findlocalweather.com, enter your zip code to find the current weather conditions, including atmospheric pressure in your area (listed as Barometer).

The pressure is reported in *inches*, so remind students that 29.9213 inches Hg = 760 mm Hg = 1 atmosphere. Also, in the interest of class time, conversions can be completed quickly at: http://www.onlineconversion.com/pressure.htm

The adjustment for the vapor pressure of water is not included in these lab directions; however, if you want to include it for accuracy (which can improve results), there's room in the data table for it to be added.

A list of vapor pressure versus water temperatures is at:
http://intro.chem.okstate.edu/1515sp01/database/vpwater.html .

You might want to perform the calculations for one trial as a class. You could also collect molar volume results from all the groups so the class has access to several trial results.

> ***Safety**
> Remove flames or other ignition sources from the laboratory. Students should not be allowed to ignite the lighters.

Class Materials:
Butane lighters   Graduated cylinders or plastic baby bottles
balance   large beakers or buckets large enough to submerge baby bottles
thermometers   (if necessary, submerge bottles on their side to fit under water)

Materials for the teacher:
Waterproof marker for labeling   Sign-out sheet and pen/pencil

Preparation:
You may want to label the butane lighters and have students sign them out and sign the lighter in when they return if. Since the butane lighter is an item that is small and easily taken out of the classroom, this is a way to make sure it is returned and to give you a paper trail if a butane lighter is missing.

During lab:
A good portion of your time could be spent signing out and in the butane lighters. When not doing that, circulate to answer questions and make sure the lighters are being used properly.

Pages to use for "Molar Volume":
10 question report: pages 77-78.
Full write-up: pages 80-81.

Possible ChemMatters article:
Graham, Tim, "Unusual Sunken Treasure", ChemMatters, December, 2006, pp.11-13, American Chemical Society.

This article describes how bottles of champagne from a ship that sunk in 1918 were brought to the surface safely, as well as how the gaseous wine is produced.

Directions of how to get the article online are on Page 2.

Sources:

http://serendip.brynmawr.edu/sci_edu/farber/pdf/bic.pdf

http://www.cpet.ufl.edu/BestPractices/PDF/Physical%20Science/Properties%20of%20Matter/Experimentally%20determine%20the%20molar%20mass%20of%20Butane%20lab.pdf

http://dwb4.unl.edu/Chemistry/dochem/DoChem077.html

http://cpet.ufl.edu/BestPractices/PDF/Physical%20Science/Properties%20of%20Matter/General%20gas%20law%20used%20to%20calculate%20partial%20pressure%20and%20molecular%20weight%20of%20butane%20gas.pdf

http://staff.fcps.net/JSWANGO/unit5/gases/Determining%20the%20Molar%20Mass%20of%20Butane.pdf

http://www.apsu.edu/ROBERTSONR/Chem1020/Butanelabrev.pdf

http://www.findlocalweather.com

http://www.onlineconversion.com/pressure.htm

http://intro.chem.okstate.edu/1515sp01/database/vpwater.html

Holt ChemFile Mini-Guide to Problem Solving, Austin, TX Holt, Rinehart and Winston, 1998.

Graham, Tim, "Unusual Sunken Treasure", ChemMatters, October, 2006, pp.11-13, American Chemical Society.

Lab: Molar Volume   Name _____

Purpose:
To collect a sample of butane gas (C_4H_{10}) and determine its molar volume (liter/mole) at standard temperature and pressure (STP).

Materials:
butane lighter   plastic baby bottle   thermometer
graduated cylinder   large beaker or bucket   balance

Safety:
Do NOT operate lab burners or other ignition sources during this lab.
Students are NOT allowed to ignite the lighters.

Procedure:
1. Hold the lighter under water for 30 seconds. Remove and shake lighter to remove excess water. Dry lighter, mass and record.
2. Fill a large beaker about ¾ full with water. Immerse the baby bottle in the water and fill to the top with water. Position the bottle so it's upside-down in the water and completely filled with water (no air bubbles). It's OK if the bottle sticks out of the water, just make sure the open end is under water.
3. Hold the lighter under the opening of the bottle. Press the release valve to release the butane gas. Collect several hundred milliliters of gas.
4. Adjust the bottle until the water level inside and outside is the same, and record the volume of gas collected. (This adjustment is to make sure the pressure inside the bottle is the same as the atmospheric pressure outside).
5. Remove the lighter and dry. Mass the dried lighter and record.
6. Measure and record the temperature of the water.
7. Record the atmospheric pressure of the room.
8. Finally, fill the baby bottle with water to the volume of the butane gas collected. Pour the water into a graduated cylinder, measure and record its volume.

Questions
Answer these questions on your own paper. Rewrite the question or incorporate it into your answer for responses without math. For all mathematical questions, show your work including units.
1. Using the combined gas law ($P_1V_1/T_1 = P_2V_2/T_2$), calculate the volume (V_2) of the gas at standard temperature and pressure (STP). Report the gas volume in liters (convert the milliliters to liters).
2. For one trial, convert the mass of butane (C_4H_{10}) collected to moles.
3. For one trial, calculate the molar volume (Liter/mole) at STP.
4. For both trials, calculate the percent error of the molar volume value at STP.
5. Evaluate the quality of your results based on your percent error values.
6. Describe how you would improve this lab using the same materials.
7. A laboratory sample of hydrogen occupies a volume of 655 mL at a pressure of 0.965 atm. What volume will the gas occupy at a pressure of 1.25 atm and at the same temperature?
8. A helium balloon contains a volume of 1500. mL at a temperature of 22.0 °C. What volume will the gas in the balloon have at 45.0 °C?
9. A gas cylinder of argon has a pressure of 3.14 atm at 22.0 °C. At what Celsius temperature will it reach a pressure of 5.00 atm?
10. A sample of oxygen gas has a volume of 50.0 mL at a pressure of 0.990 atm and a temperature of 20.0 °C. What volume will the oxygen occupy at 0.890 atm and 25.0 °?

Data – Trial 1

Initial mass of lighter (g)	
Final mass of lighter (g)	
Mass of gas (g)	
Volume of gas (mL)	
Temperature of gas (°C)	
Pressure of gas (atm)	
Volume of gas at STP (L)	
Moles of gas (mol)	
Lab value of molar volume (L/mol)	
Percent error of molar volume (%)	

Data – Trial 2

Initial mass of lighter (g)	
Final mass of lighter (g)	
Mass of gas (g)	
Volume of gas (mL)	
Temperature of gas (°C)	
Pressure of gas (atm)	
Volume of gas at STP (L)	
Moles of gas (mol)	
Lab value of molar volume (L/mol)	
Percent error of molar volume (%)	

Answer Key for "Molar Volume":

Sample data used for questions # 1 through #4.

Mass of lighter before = 125.00 g

- Mass of lighter after = 124.70 g

Mass of gas = 0.30 g

Volume of gas (mL) = 100.0 ml = V_1

Temperature of gas (°C) = 25.0 °C + 273K
= 298.0 K = T_1

Pressure of gas (atm) = 1.05 atm = P_1

1. $$\frac{P_1 V_1}{T_1} = \frac{P_2 V_2}{T_2} \rightarrow \frac{P_1 V_1 T_2}{P_2 T_1} = V_2$$

   At STP → T_2 = 0 °C = 273 K and P_2 = 1.00 atm

   $$\frac{(273 \text{ K} \times 1.05 \text{ atm} \times 100.0 \text{ ml})}{(1.00 \text{ atm} \times 298.0 \text{ K})} = 96.2 \text{ mL} \times \frac{1L}{1000 \text{ mL}} = 0.0962 \text{ L}$$

2. Molar Mass C_4H_{10} = 4 (12) + 10 (1) = 58 g

   mass of gas x 1 mole /gram formula mass

   0.30 g x 1 mol / 58 g = 0.0052 mol C_4H_{10} gas

3. molar volume at STP = calculated V_2 / moles of gas collected
   = 0.0962 L / 0.0052 mol = 18.5 L/mol

4. measured value molar volume at STP = 18.5 L/mol
   accepted value molar volume at STP = 22.4 L/mol

   % error = | measured value – accepted value | / accepted value x 100%

   % error = | 18.5 L/mol – 22.4 L/mol | / 22.4 L/moL x 100%
   = 3.9 L/mol / 22.4 L/mol x 100% = 17.4% error

5. Answer depends on laboratory data, but it should reflect the percent error values.

6. Answers will vary, but possibilities are (a) to use a more accurate gas collection device such as a graduated cylinder or (b) to stabilize the gas collection device by clamping it to a ring stand.

7. $P_1 V_1 = P_2 V_2$ → (655 mL x 0.965 atm) / 1.25 atm = 506 mL = V_2

8. $V_1/T_1 = V_2/T_2$ → $V_1 \times T_2 / T_1$ → (1500. mL x 318 K) / 295 K = 1617 mL

9. $P_1/T_1 = P_2/T_2$ → $P_1 \times T_2 = P_2 \times T_1$ → ($P_2 \times T_1$) / P_1 = (5.00 atm x 295 K) / 3.14 atm = 470. K

   470. K – 273 K = 197 °C

10. $P_1 V_1/T_1 = P_2 V_2/T_2$ → ($T_2 \times P_1 \times V_1$)/ ($P_2 \times T_1$) →

    (298 K x 0.990 atm x 50.0 mL) / (0.890 atm x 293 K) = 56.6 mL

Lab: Molar Volume   Name _____

Purpose:
To collect a sample of butane gas (C_4H_{10}) and determine its molar volume (liter/mole) at standard temperature and pressure (STP).

Materials:
butane lighters   plastic baby bottles   thermometer
graduated cylinders   large beaker or buckets   balance

Safety
Do NOT operate lab burners or other ignition sources during this lab.
Students are NOT allowed to ignite the lighters.

Procedure:
1. Hold the lighter under water for 30 seconds. Remove and shake lighter to remove excess water. Dry lighter, mass and record.
2. Fill a large beaker about ¾ full with water. Immerse the baby bottle in the water and fill to the top with water. Position the bottle so it's upside-down in the water and completely filled with water (no air bubbles). It's OK if the bottle sticks out of the water, just make sure the open end is under water.
3. Hold the lighter under the opening of the bottle. Press the valve to release the butane gas. Collect several hundred milliliters of gas.
4. Adjust the bottle until the water level inside and outside is the same, and record the volume of gas collected. (This adjustment is to make sure the pressure inside the bottle is the same as the atmospheric pressure outside).
5. Remove the lighter and dry. Mass the dried lighter and record.
6. Measure and record the temperature of the water.
7. Record the atmospheric pressure of the room.
8. Finally, fill the baby bottle with water to the volume of the butane gas collected. Pour the water into a graduated cylinder, measure and record its volume.

Laboratory Report Requirements
Label and skip a line between each section. Label when data tables and charts are attached on separate pages (ex. Data Table – see attached.)
Title, Purpose, Materials, Procedure

Calculations (for one trial)
1. Using the combined gas law ($P_1V_1/T_1 = P_2V_2/T_2$), calculate the volume (V_2) of the gas at standard temperature and pressure. Report the gas volume in liters (convert the milliliters to liters).
2. Convert the mass of butane gas collected to moles. Show your work including units.
3. Calculate the molar volume (mole/Liter) of the gas collected at STP. Show your work including units.
4. Calculate the percent error of the two measured molar volume values. Show your work including units.

Conclusion
In paragraph form, discuss the following ideas:
- Evaluate the quality of your results based on your percent error values.
- Describe how you would improve this lab using the same materials.
- Using Kinetic Molecular Theory, describe what must change for 1 mole of gas to increase in volume, pressure and temperature.
- A sample of oxygen gas has a volume of 50.0 mL at a pressure of 0.990 atm and a temperature of 20.0 °C. What volume will the oxygen occupy at 0.890 atm and 25.0 °C?

Data – Trial 1

Initial mass of lighter (g)	
Final mass of lighter (g)	
Mass of gas (g)	
Volume of gas (mL)	
Temperature of gas (°C)	
Pressure of gas (atm)	
Volume of gas at STP (L)	
Moles of gas (mol)	
Lab value of molar volume (L/mol)	
Percent error of molar volume (%)	

Data – Trial 2

Initial mass of lighter (g)	
Final mass of lighter (g)	
Mass of gas (g)	
Volume of gas (mL)	
Temperature of gas (°C)	
Pressure of gas (atm)	
Volume of gas at STP (L)	
Moles of gas (mol)	
Lab value of molar volume (L/mol)	
Percent error of molar volume (%)	

Lab: Heat of Fusion

Summary
Student measures volume and temperature of a sample of warm water. Ice is added and the mixture is allowed to reach its lowest temperature. The temperature and volume of the remaining water is measured. The heat of fusion of water is calculated.

Student Skills:
Performance of the laboratory technique of calorimetry
Calculation of percent error

Lab: Heat of Fusion — Teacher Information Page

Background:
Students find this experiment interesting because they can easily determine the quality of their results. The materials are very simple to gather but thermometers are necessary to perform this lab. If you don't have enough thermometers, check with the other teachers in the science department to see if you can borrow any.

> **Remember:** The density of H_2O = 1 g/ml, so by measuring the volume you can determine the mass easily. For example, 100 ml of water equals 100 g of water. Students don't always recognize this, so you may want to remind them.

The energy lost by warm water cooling is equal to the energy gained to melt the ice and to warm the water produced:

$$m_{warm\ water}\ c\ \Delta T_{warm\ water} = m_{ice\ melted}\ H_f + m_{ice\ melted}\ c\ \Delta T_{ice\ water}$$

The calculations in the question section are presented in two parts so that students don't get overwhelmed. You may want to complete these calculations as a class.

Class Materials:
Large Styrofoam cups (473 mL or 16 oz.)
Graduated cylinders
Thermometers

Access to warm water
Ice
Tongs or spoon

Materials for the teacher:
Nothing!

Preparation:
A bag or two of ice cubes can be purchased at the local grocery store. You may have to locate a freezer for the storage of the ice -- a cooler can be handy for storing the ice in the classroom during the lab.

Hot water from the tap is warm enough for this lab.

During lab:
Circulate to observe students working and aid as necessary.

Pages to use for "Heat of Fusion":
10 question report: pages 85-86.
Full write-up: pages 88-89.

Possible ChemMatters article:
Ruth, Carolyn, "Letting Off Steam", ChemMatters, April, 2009, pp.4-7, American Chemical Society.

This article describes the chemistry of geysers and superheated water underground at high pressures.

Directions of how to get the article online are on Page 2.

Another fun article related to the topic of heat is:
Rohrig, Brian, "Thermometers", ChemMatters, December, 2006, pp. 14-17, American Chemical Society.
This article describes the historical development of thermometers and temperature scales.

Sources:

http://boomeria.org/labsphys/physlabook/lab20.pdf

http://fay.basd.k12.wi.us/page2/Heat%20of%20Fusion.pdf

http://www.dbooth.net/mhs/chem/icefusion.html

http://www2.bakersfieldcollege.edu/dkimball/Physical%20Science/New%20Labs/Exp%204%20Heat%20of%20Fusion-Melting%20Ice.pdf

http://science.csustan.edu/CHEM1112_4/calorimetry/CalorimetryandCoffeeCups.pdf

Ruth, Carolyn, "Letting Off Steam", ChemMatters, April, 2009, pp.4-7, American Chemical Society.

Rohrig, Brian, "Thermometers", ChemMatters, December, 2006, pp. 14-17, American Chemical Society.

Lab: Heat of Fusion

Name _____

Purpose: To use calorimetry to calculate the Heat of Fusion of H_2O.

Materials:
Large Styrofoam cups
Access to warm water
Ice
Thermometers
Graduated cylinders
Tongs or a spoon

WARNING: Thermometers break easily! Keep them away from the edges of the table. Do NOT leave them unattended in a beaker or cup.

Procedure:

1. Let the tap water run to get the hottest water possible. Place 100 mL of hot water into a Styrofoam cup. Record the exact volume of the water and its temperature.

2. Obtain ice cubes. Shake off any excess water from their surface or dry with a paper towel.

3. Place the ice in the warm water and stir the mixture until the temperature is 0-5 °C. Add more ice if needed to cool the water.

4. When you have reached the lowest temperature, remove any unmelted ice with tongs or a spoon. Let as much water as possible drip from the pieces of ice into the water in the cup. Record the lowest temperature reached.

5. Measure the total volume of water in the calorimeter. You may have to fill your graduated cylinder more than once.

Data: Remember: the density of H_2O = 1 g/ml

Mass of warm water (g) _____

Temperature of warm water (°C) _____

Final temperature of ice-water (°C) _____

Final mass of ice-water (g) _____

Initial temperature of ice (°C) _____

Final temperature of ice-water (°C) _____

Specific heat capacity of water = 1 cal / (g °C) = 4.18 J / (g °C)

Questions

Answer these questions on your own paper using full sentences -- either rewrite the question or incorporate it into your answer.

1. Explain how energy was transferred so that hot water temperature changed and the ice melted.

2. State the Law of Conservation of Energy.

3. Determine the mass of ice that melted. Remember that the density of water is 1.00 g/mL.

4. Calculate the energy released by the warm water in the calorimeter both in calories and joules. Show your work with units.

$$Energy_{released} = mass_{hot\ water} \times specific\ heat_{water} \times \Delta T_{hot\ water}$$

5. Solve for the Heat of Fusion (H_f) in calories/gram$_{ice}$ based on your lab measurements -- show your work with units.

$$Energy_{released} = Energy_{absorbed} = (H_f \times mass_{ice}) + (mass_{ice} \times specific\ heat_{water} \times \Delta T_{ice\ water})$$

6. Solve for the Heat of Fusion (H_f) in joules/grams$_{ice}$ based on your lab measurements. Show your work with units.

$$Energy_{released} = Energy_{absorbed} = (H_f \times mass_{ice}) + (mass_{ice} \times specific\ heat_{water} \times \Delta T_{ice\ water})$$

7. Calculate the percent error of both trial results for Heat of Fusion in cal/g. Show your work with units.

8. Calculate the percent error for both trials results for Heat of Fusion in J/g. Show your work with units.

9. Evaluate the quality of your results.

10. Describe how you would improve this lab using the same or similar materials.

Answer Key for "Heat of Fusion":

1. Energy left the hot water, which is why its temperature reduced, and went into the ice, causing the ice to melt and the resulting water to increase in temperature.

2. According to the Law of Conservation of Energy, energy is neither created nor destroyed. In this lab, the amount of energy lost by the warm water is equal to the amount of energy used to melt the ice and warm the resulting water.

3. $Volume_{ice\ water} = Volume_{final\ (cool\ water)} - Volume_{initial\ (warm\ water)}$

   Since the density of H_2O = 1 g/ml,

   $Mass_{ice} = Mass_{final\ (cool\ water)} - Mass_{initial\ (warm\ water)}$

4. Sample problem:

   $Q = mc\Delta T$

   $Q = 100\ g \times 1\ cal/(g \cdot °C) \times 10\ °C = 1000\ cal$

   $Q = 100\ g \times 4.18\ J/(g \cdot °C) \times 10\ °C = 4180\ J$

5. $1000\ cal = (H_f \times 10\ g) + (10\ g \times 1\ cal/(g \cdot °C) \times 5\ °C)$

   $1000\ cal = (H_f \times 10\ g) + 50\ cal$
   $-\ 50\ cal \qquad\qquad -\ 50\ cal$

   $950\ cal\ /\ 10\ g = (H_f \times 10\ g)\ /\ 10\ g$

   $H_f = 95\ cal/g$

6. $4180\ J = (H_f \times 10\ g) + (10\ g \times 4.18\ J/(g \cdot °C) \times 5\ °C)$

   $4180\ J = (H_f \times 10\ g) + 209\ J$
   $-\ 209\ J \qquad\qquad -\ 209\ J$

   $3971\ J\ /\ 10\ g = (H_f \times 10\ g)\ /\ 10\ g$

   397 J/g

7. (95 cal/g − 80 cal/g) / 80 cal/g × 100 % = 19 % error

8. (397 J/g − 334 J/g) / 334 J/g × 100 % = 19 % error

9. Several answers apply but should correlate with the reported percent error value.

10. Several answers apply. One possibility is to use a lid on the Styrofoam cup to prevent energy gain or loss from the system. Some students might mention using a *real* calorimeter but that is not using the same materials.

Lab: Heat of Fusion   **Name** _____

Purpose: To use calorimetry to calculate the Heat of Fusion of H_2O.

Materials:
Large Styrofoam cups   Ice   Graduated cylinders
Access to warm water   Thermometers   Tongs or a spoon

> **WARNING: Thermometers break easily! Keep them away from the edges of the table. Do NOT leave them unattended in a beaker or cup.**

Procedure:

1. Let the tap water run to get the hottest water possible. Place 100 mL of hot water into a Styrofoam cup. Record the exact volume of the water and its temperature.

2. Obtain ice cubes. Shake off any excess water from their surface or dry with a paper towel.

3. Place the ice in the warm water and stir the mixture until the temperature is 0-5°C. Add more ice if needed to cool the water.

4. When you have reached the lowest temperature, remove any unmelted ice with tongs or a spoon. Let as much water as possible drip from the pieces of ice into the water in the cup. Record the lowest temperature reached.

5. Measure the total volume of water in the calorimeter. You may have to fill your graduated cylinder more than once.

Data: Remember: the density of H_2O = 1 g/ml

Mass of warm water (g)   _____

Temperature of warm water (°C)   _____

Final temperature of ice-water (°C)   _____

Final mass of ice-water (g)   _____

Initial temperature of ice (°C)   _____

Final temperature of ice-water (°C)   _____

Specific heat capacity of water = 1 cal / (g · °C) = 4.18 J / (g °C)

Laboratory Report Requirements

Label and skip a line between each section. Data tables and charts attached on separate pages are to be labeled (ex. Data Table – see attached).

Title

Purpose

Materials

Procedure

Data

Calculations

1. Determine the mass of ice that melted. Assume that the density of water is 1.00 g/mL.

2. Calculate the energy released by the warm water initially in the calorimeter both in calories and joules.

$$\text{Energy}_{released} = \text{mass}_{hot\,water} \times \text{specific heat}_{water} \times \Delta T_{hot\,water}$$

3. Solve for the Heat of Fusion (H_f) in calories/gram$_{ice}$ based on your lab measurements.

$$\text{Energy}_{released} = \text{Energy}_{absorbed} = (H_f \times \text{mass}_{ice}) + (\text{mass}_{ice} \times \text{specific heat}_{water} \times \Delta T_{ice\,water})$$

4. Solve for the Heat of Fusion (H_f) in joules/gram$_{ice}$ based on your lab measurements.

5. Calculate the percent error of both trials of your measured Heats of Fusion in J/g.

Conclusion

In paragraph form, discuss the following ideas:

- Explain how energy was transferred so that hot water temperature changed and the ice melted.

- State the Law of Conservation of Energy.

- Evaluate the quality of your results.

- Describe how you would improve this lab using the same or similar materials.

Lab: Calorimetry

Summary:
Student heats up a measured volume of water with a candle. The temperature of the water and mass of the candle are measured before and after heating. Using the formula $Q = mc\Delta T$, the student calculates the energy released by the candle. The joule/gram of candle wax is also calculated.

Students can work in pairs to conserve materials.

Student Skills:
Performance of the laboratory technique of calorimetry
Calculation of percent error

Lab: Calorimetry — Teacher Information Page

Background:
This lab is helpful in showing students how energy is measured once it is released from its source. I have reminded my students that we don't have an instrument to measure the energy in something, but that we have to *release the energy as heat* and heat up a substance with a known specific heat value such as water.

Over the years, I have performed this lab with various fuel sources. Peanuts can be mounted on needles which have been stuck into large corks (such as size 7 or 8). The only problem is that oil drips from the peanuts and the sometimes the corks catch on fire (oops), so those corks can't be used for anything else.

Cheese puffs (or cheese doodles) light rather easily, and can be held with crucible tongs under a small beaker mounted in a clamp attached to a ring stand. It is fascinating for students to observe the food that they eat actually burn, but it's a very smelly and dirty lab to perform. The ash from the food gets on everything!

Tea-light candles are inexpensive, stand on their own, and are easily obtained, so this is the fuel source used in this lab.

This lab will have a very high percent error. The set-up was chosen for two reasons: (1) so that students could easily observe the flow of energy from the candle to the water, and (2) so that students could analyze possible sources of heat loss. Sometimes students have to perform a lab with poor results to realize the need for reflection and redesign to improve results.

Attaching the candles to index cards makes it easier to mass the candles before and after performing the lab.

To fix the candle to an index card, light the candle and drip some of its melted wax onto the card. Then place the candle on the melted wax. When the wax cools and hardens, the candle will be stuck to the card.

Remember melted wax is hot and burns skin! Remind students **not** to walk around with melted candles!

Lab thermometers are necessary to perform this lab. If you don't have enough thermometers, check with the other teachers in the science department to see if you can borrow any.

You may wish to guide the students through the calculations for one trial to prevent confusion.

Class Materials:

tea-light candles	beaker (100 mL)	wire gauze	matches
ring	graduated cylinder	balance	
index cards	ring stand	thermometer	

Materials for the teacher:
Nothing!

Preparation:
You may wish to cut the index cards in half ahead of time because you don't need to use a whole card for one candle.

During lab:
Circulate to observe students working and aid as necessary.

Pages to use for "Calorimetry":
10 question report: pages 93-94 and 95 for a data page.
Full write-up: pages 97-98 and 99 for a data page.

Possible ChemMatters article:
Tinnesand, Michael, "A Single Ignition: A Cautionary Tale", ChemMatters, April, 2011, pp.10-11, American Chemical Society.

This article describes the explosion of a crude oil storage tank.

This article is also a good supplement for the topics of **Fractional Distillation** and **Reaction Rates**.

Directions of how to get the article online are on Page 2.

Sources:

Orna, Schreck and Heikkinen, Chemsource: Instructional Resources for Preservice and Inservice Chemistry Teachers, Volume 4, ChemSource, Inc., 1994. (Thermochemistry chapter, pp. 7-14)

http://www.chalkbored.com/lessons/chemistry-11/candle-lab.pdf

http://www.lopezlink.com/Labs/Calorimetry%20Lab/calorimetry%20lab.htm

http://www.wolfcreek.ab.ca/HIA/Documents/Division%20IV/Measuring%20Calories2.pdf

http://galileo.phys.virginia.edu/outreach/8thGradeSOL/FuelEnergyFrm.htm

Wilbraham, Antony et al., Chemistry, Fifth Edition, Prentice Hall, 2000.

Tinnesand, Michael, "A Single Ignition: A Cautionary Tale", ChemMatters, April, 2011, pp.10-11, American Chemical Society.

Lab: Calorimetry   Name _____

Purpose: To use calorimetry to measure the joule/gram of the candle wax.

Materials:
tea-light candles   beaker (100 mL)   wire gauze   balance
matches   ring   graduated cylinder   thermometer
index cards   ring stand

WARNING: Thermometers break easily! Keep them away from the edges of the table. Do not leave them unattended in a beaker or cup.

SAFETY: Goggles are required during this lab.

Procedure:

1. Set up lab apparatus according to this diagram →

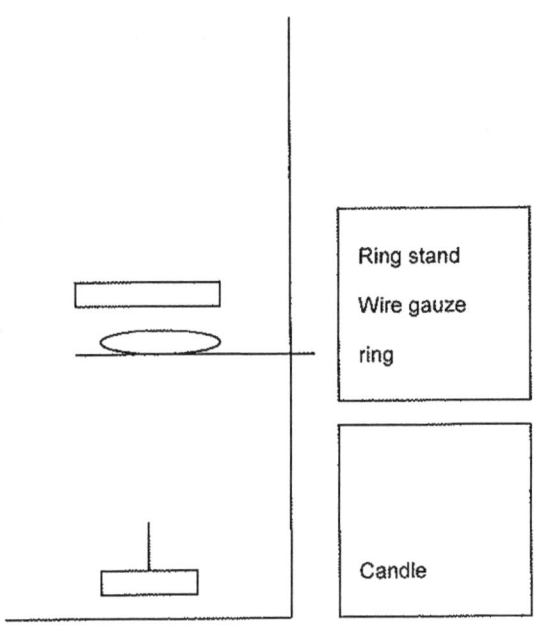

2. Light the candle and let some melted wax drip onto the index card. Blow out the candle and set it on the hot wax to fix it to the card.

3. Measure 50 mL of water and place into the beaker.

4. Measure the initial temperature of the water and the mass of the candle + card.

5. Set the beaker on top of the wire gauze on the ring/ring stand setup.

6. Put the candle on the base of the ring stand. Light candle and let burn for 5 minutes.

7. Extinguish the candle flame. Measure the highest water temperature. Measure final mass of candle + card. <u>Careful:</u> the candle wax is melted and can spill!

8. Repeat steps #2-5. Cool the beaker or use another room temperature beaker.

Data: Table attached.

Questions

Answer these questions on your own paper using full sentences -- either rewrite the question or incorporate it into your answer.

Use your second trial to answer questions #1 - #5:

1. Calculate the mass of water used (Remember: the density of water is 1 g/mL).

2. Calculate the mass of candle wax burned.

3. Calculate the heat absorbed by the water (c_{H2O} = 4.18 J/g°C).

4. Calculate the amount of heat released per gram of wax (J/g).

5. The heat of combustion for paraffin wax is 42.0 kJ/g. How many J/g is that? Calculate the percent error for the measured J/g.

6. Explain why you divided the joules measured by the change in the mass of the candle.

7. In question #3 above, 4.18 J/g°C was used as the specific heat capacity of the calorimeter. Suggest a reason why this is not entirely accurate.

8. Evaluate the quality of your results.

9. Describe how you would improve this lab using the same or similar materials.

10. Paraffin wax has the formula $C_{25}H_{52}$. Write a balanced chemical equation, including phases, for the combustion of liquid paraffin wax.

Data Trial 1

Initial mass of candle and card (g)	
Final mass of candle and card (g)	
Mass of wax burned (g)	
Initial temperature of water (°C)	
Final temperature of water (°C)	
ΔT (°C)	
Amount of heat released by candle (J)	
Joules/gram of candle (J/g)	
Percent Error (%)	

Data Trial 2

Initial mass of candle and card (g)	
Final mass of candle and card (g)	
Mass of wax burned (g)	
Initial temperature of water (°C)	
Final temperature of water (°C)	
ΔT (°C)	
Amount of heat released by candle (J)	
Joules/gram of candle (J/g)	
Percent Error (%)	

Answer Key for "Calorimetry":

Sample data is used for questions #1 - #5:

1. 50 mL x 1 g/mL = 50 g

2. 200 g – 190 g = 10 g

3. Heat water absorbed = mcΔT = 50g x 4.18 J/g°C x 8 °C = 1672 J = Heat released by candle

4. 1672 J / 10 g = 167.2 J/g

5. 42.0 kJ/g x 1000J/kJ = 42 000 J/g

   $$\frac{|42\,000 \text{ J/g} - 167.2 \text{ J/g}|}{42\,000 \text{ J/g}} \times 100\% = 99.6\% \text{ error}$$

   The values will be large, some as large as 200% !

6. Different amounts of candle wax were burned in each trial, so to be able to compare the results, the value is reduced to joules per gram of wax burned.

7. The beaker containing the water was also heated, so taking into account the mass of the beaker and its specific heat value (0.50 J/g °C or 0.12 cal/g °C) accounts for more of the heat released.

8. Several answers apply but should correlate with the reported percent error value.

9. Several answers apply, but usually students suggest use of some sort of insulated or closed system.

10. $C_{25}H_{52}$ (l) + 38 O_2 (g) → 25 CO_2 (g) + 26 H_2O (g)

Lab: Calorimetry   Name _____

Purpose: To use calorimetry to measure the joule/gram of the candle wax.

Materials:
tea-light candles	beaker (100 mL)	wire gauze	balance
matches	ring	graduated cylinder	thermometer
index cards	ring stand		

WARNING: Thermometers break easily! Keep them away from the edges of the table. Do not leave them unattended in a beaker or cup.

SAFETY: Goggles are required during this lab.

Procedure:

1. Set up lab apparatus according to this diagram →

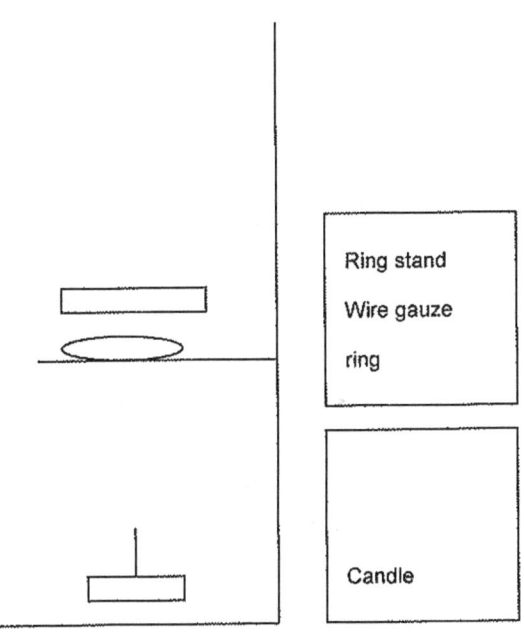

2. Light the candle and let some melted wax drip onto the index card. Blow out the candle and set it on the hot wax to fix it to the card.

3. Measure 50 mL of water and place into the beaker.

4. Measure the initial temperature of the water and the mass of the candle + card.

5. Set the beaker on top of the wire gauze on the ring/ring stand setup.

6. Put the candle on the base of the ring stand. Light candle and let burn for 5 minutes.

7. Extinguish the candle flame. Measure the highest water temperature. Measure final mass of candle + card. Careful: the candle wax is melted and can spill!

8. Repeat steps #2-5. Cool the beaker or use another room temperature beaker.

Data: Table attached.

Laboratory Report Requirements

Label and skip a line between each section. Data tables and charts attached on separate pages are to be labeled (ex. Data Table – see attached).

Title

Purpose

Materials

Procedure

Data

Sample Calculation for Trial Two

1. Mass of water used (Remember: the density of water is 1 g/mL).

2. Mass of candle wax burned.

3. Heat absorbed by the water (assume (c_{H2O} = 4.18 J/g°C).

4. Heat released per gram of wax (J/g).

5. The heat of combustion for paraffin wax is 42.0 kJ/g. How many J/g is that? Calculate the percent error for the measured J/g.

Conclusion
In paragraph form, discuss the following ideas:

- Paraffin wax has the formula $C_{25}H_{52}$. Write a balanced chemical equation including phases for the combustion of liquid paraffin wax.

- In calculation #3, 4.18 J/g°C was used as the specific heat capacity of the calorimeter. Suggest a reason why this is not entirely accurate.

- Evaluate the quality of your results.

- Describe how you would improve this lab using the same or similar materials.

Data Trial 1

Initial mass of candle and card (g)	
Final mass of candle and card (g)	
Mass of wax burned (g)	
Initial temperature of water (°C)	
Final temperature of water (°C)	
ΔT (°C)	
Amount of heat released by candle (J)	
Joules/gram of candle (J/g)	
Percent Error (%)	

Data Trial 2

Initial mass of candle and card (g)	
Final mass of candle and card (g)	
Mass of wax burned (g)	
Initial temperature of water (°C)	
Final temperature of water (°C)	
ΔT (°C)	
Amount of heat released by candle (J)	
Joules/gram of candle (J/g)	
Percent Error (%)	

Lab: Household Acids & Bases

Summary
Student uses different acid-base indicators to test various substances. Students work in groups of two to four students.

Student Skills:
Use of various acid-base indicators
Identification of acidic, basic and neutral substances

Lab: Household Acids & Bases — Teacher Information Page

Background:
This lab tests pH using stirring rods, indicator papers and spot plates.
What if you don't have spot plates? Plastic spot plates are available through laboratory or photographic supply companies, but they can be costly. You may want to check with the biology or earth science teachers to see if spot plates are available.

A half-sheet of a plastic overhead can be used instead of a spot plate. If the indicator is in liquid form, the mixing of substance and indicator can occur directly on the overhead sheet. Conveniently, the overhead could be placed over the data chart, and mixing would occur directly on the plastic, and then the page is slid away to write down the results.

You might want to set up stations where the substance to be tested is in a small, plastic bowl. Each station would have indicator papers/solutions available or the student would carry a supply of fresh papers. In the place of spot plates, a student could use a piece of plastic overhead to carry with them to provide a surface on which to work.

Students are NOT to dip the papers directly into the sample. Samples can end up mixed and the pH results would not be accurate. Instruct students to dip a clean stirring rod or coffee stirrer in the sample that could be used to spot the indicator paper. You may wish to provide a stirring rod with each sample to prevent cross contamination.

A full piece of indicator paper is not necessary to complete the pH test for a sample. You or your students may wish to cut or rip up the papers (4 per each 5 cm strip) to use fewer supplies.

Many class labs already have red/blue litmus papers and phenolphthalein. This lab is designed for four indicators. The specific indicators are intentionally left blank so that the indicators used can be entered.

What if your lab doesn't have any acid-base indicators? In the next lab, instructions are given for the preparation of liquid acid-base indicators from fruits and vegetables.

Food choices that are tested for pH (milk and orange juice) can be purchased that lab day in small containers -- they may even be available at the school cafeteria.

Even though the acids and bases being used are not very strong, goggles and aprons should still be worn.

Class Materials:
Various household material samples
Acid-base Indicators (ideally four)

Spot plates
Stirring rods

Materials for the teacher:
Extra indicator papers

Preparation:
Obtain the acid-base indicators that will be used.

During lab:
Circulate to observe students working and aid as necessary.

Pages to use for "Household Acids & Bases":
10 question report: page 103 and data tables on pages 104-105.
Full write-up: page 108 and data tables on pages 109-110.

Possible ChemMatters article:
Yarnell, Amanda, "Kitty Litter Chem", ChemMatters, October, 2005, pp.12-14, American Chemical Society.

This article describes the development of various cat litter choices, the requirements and limitations of kitty litter, and provides a brief diagram of the **Chemical Bonding** that occurs when the kitty litter is activated.

Directions of how to get the article online are on Page 2.

Sources:

http://www.scioptic-usa.com/posppl.html

http://www.biolady.net/labs/word_documents/acidbase_lab.pdf

http://mypages.iit.edu/~smile/ch8622.html

http://chemistry.about.com/cs/acidsandbases/a/aa060703a.htm

http://www.chem.umn.edu/services/lecturedemo/info/Cabbage_Indicator.html
This article has directions for preparing red cabbage indicator.

Snyder, Carl H. "Chapter Nine: Acids and Bases," The Extraordinary Chemistry of Ordinary Things, 3rd Edition, John Wiley & Sons, Inc., 1998.

Yarnell, Amanda, "Kitty Litter Chem" ChemMatters, October, 2005, pp.12-14, American Chemical Society.

Lab: Household Acids & Bases   Name _____

Purpose:
Identification of acids, bases and neutral substances.
Use of various acid-base indicators.

Materials:
Various sample substances   Spot plates
Acid-base Indicators   Stirring rods

Safety goggles are required.

Procedure:
Test 20 samples with all 4 acid-base indicators using a spot plate and a stirring rod.

Smaller pieces of indicator papers may be used.

The 1st ten samples are required (see chart), the next ten are your choice.

Data -- Chart attached

Questions
Answer these questions on your own paper using full sentences -- rewrite the question or incorporate it into your answer.

1. List the substances tested that were found to be acidic.

2. Generally, what type of substances were acids?

3. List the substances tested that were found to be basic.

4. Generally, what type of substances were basic?

5. List the substances tested that were found to be neutral.

6. Generally, what type of substances were neutral?

7. Describe two situations in which acid-base indicators might be useful in everyday life.

8. Suppose you are manufacturing a certain type if hand lotion. You know that it can be slightly acidic, but it should not be strongly acidic. Which of the indicators used in this lab would you use? Explain your choice.

9. Evaluate the quality of your results.

10. Describe how you would improve this lab using the same or similar materials.

Data Table 1

Substance	Indicator 1	Indicator 2	Indicator 3	Indicator 4	Acid/ base/ neutral?
0.1 M HCl					
0.1 M NH$_4$OH					
Tap water					
Distilled water					
NaCl (aq)					
NaHCO$_3$ (aq)					
Liquid hand soap					
Rubbing alcohol					
Milk					
Orange juice					

Data Table 2

Substance	Indicator 1	Indicator 2	Indicator 3	Indicator 4	Acid/ base/ neutral?

Answer Key for "Household Acids and Bases":

1. Substances found to be acidic include HCl, tap water and orange juice.

2. Generally, citrus fruits, soda or fruit juice are acids.

3. Substances found to be basic include NH_4OH, $NaHCO_3$ (aq) and cleaners.

4. Generally, cleaning products are basic.

5. Substances found to be neutral include distilled water, NaCl (aq), liquid hand soap, rubbing alcohol, milk and toothpaste.

6. Generally, substances used on human skin are neutral.

7. Answers will vary, but two examples are:

    a. Production of soap requires a reaction between a fat and lye (potassium hydroxide) – the final product should be neutral for use on human skin. It is important to test the soap produced so that it is not too basic (alkaline).

    b. A swimming pool needs to be neutral for use, but the chemicals used to clean the pool of algae and other microorganisms can cause an imbalance. Acid-base indicators are routinely used to determine the quality of pool water for swimming.

8. This answer depends on the indicators that are used. Litmus indicator does not indicate acid-base strength and is not the best choice to indicate the pH desired. An answer may include a combination of acid-base indicators.

9. Answers will vary. Possible responses include concerns about the accuracy or consistency of the homemade acid-base indicators or concerns about cross contamination of samples.

10. Answers will vary. Possible responses include preparing fresh batches of the lab-made acid-base indicator or using personal samples of acid-base indicator to prevent contamination.

Sample Answers for Data Table 1

Substance	Red Litmus Indicator 1	Blue Litmus Indicator 2	Red Cabbage Indicator 3	Onion Skin Indicator 4	Acid/ base/ neutral?
0.1 M HCl	Red	Red	Red	Brown/orange	Acid
0.1 M NH$_4$OH	Blue	Blue	Green	Yellow/orange	Base
Tap water	Red	Blue	Purple	Brown/orange	Neutral
Distilled water	Red	Blue	Purple	Brown/orange	Neutral
NaCl (aq)	Red	Blue	Purple	Brown/orange	Neutral
NaHCO$_3$ (aq)	Blue	Blue	Blue	Orange	Base
Liquid hand soap	Red	Blue	Purple	Brown/orange	Neutral
Isopropyl alcohol	Red	Blue	Purple	Brown/orange	Neutral
Milk	Red	Red	Purple	Brown/orange	Neutral
Orange juice	Red	Red	Red	Brown/orange	Acid

Lab: Household Acids & Bases   Name _____

Purpose:
Identification of acids, bases and neutral substances.
Use of various acid-base indicators.

Materials:
Various sample substances   Spot plates
Acid-base Indicators   Stirring rods

Safety goggles are required.

Procedure:
Test 20 samples with all 4 acid-base indicators using a spot plate and a stirring rod.

Smaller pieces of indicator papers may be used.

The 1st ten samples are required (see chart), the next ten are your choice.

Laboratory Report Requirements

Label and skip a line between each section. Data tables and charts attached on separate pages are to be labeled (ex. Data Table – see attached).

Title, Purpose, Materials, Procedure

Data – Attach a completed data chart.

Conclusion
In paragraph form, discuss the following ideas:

- Write three lists of the substances tested, (1) acidic materials, (2) basic materials and (3) neutral materials.

- Generally, what type of substances were acids, bases and neutral?

- Evaluate the quality of your results. Describe how you would improve this lab using the same or similar materials.

- Suppose you are manufacturing a certain type of hand lotion. You know that it can be slightly acidic, but it should not be strongly acidic. Which of the indicators used in this lab would you use? Explain your choice.

Data Table 1

Substance	Indicator 1	Indicator 2	Indicator 3	Indicator 4	Acid/ base/ neutral?
0.1 M HCl					
0.1 M NH₄OH					
Tap water					
Distilled water					
NaCl (aq)					
NaHCO₃ (aq)					
Liquid hand soap					
Rubbing alcohol					
Milk					
Orange juice					

Data Table 2

Substance	Indicator 1	Indicator 2	Indicator 3	Indicator 4	Acid/ base/ neutral?

Lab: Preparing pH Indicators

Summary
Student prepares an acid-base indicator by boiling a fruit or vegetable to extract its pigment. The indicator color range is determined by testing it with an acid and a base.

Student Skills:
Preparation of acid-base indicator solutions for laboratory use

Lab: Preparing pH Indicators   **Teacher Information Page**

Background:

What if your lab doesn't have any acid-base indicators? It is possible to prepare acid-base indicators from fruits and vegetables. The instructor can prepare them, the students can prepare them as another lab, or students can prepare them after school to earn extra credit.

Be forewarned that these natural indicators don't last forever and eventually will show signs of mold. After you're finished using them, flush them down the sink. If you can refrigerate them they might last a little longer, but not forever. Freezing appears to work but may not be worth the effort.

These indicators are prepared in water. Alcohol is frequently used for indicator preparation to prevent mold. Alcohol is flammable and was not used in this preparation because of that danger.

Fruits and vegetables that can be used include:

Beets (canned, use the juice, too!)   Onion skins (brown, outer skins)
Blackberries (frozen OK)   *Red Cabbage
Blueberries (frozen OK)   Red Radishes
Carrots   Red Raspberries (frozen OK)
Grapes (red and purple)   Strawberries (frozen OK)

> **Red cabbage** produces a full spectrum of colors similar to universal indicator – it's worth preparing!

Flower petals can provide good indicators. Due to availability and cost they were not used.

The procedure is simply boiling the substance to extract its pigment. The choice of heat source can be tricky. The ideal is a hot plate and a beaker because it's a very stable setup. That may not be available, however, which puts you back to the traditional ring stand/ring/wire gauze with a Bunsen burner. I have had this set-up get knocked over by a student, but his rubberized lab apron protected him. Be careful!

A second day for the lab is to observe the prepared indicators alone and in acid and base solutions.

The lab handout consists of only a one-page direction and data sheet because these indicators are meant for the "Household Acids & Bases" lab. To make this assignment longer, the teacher could add a student essay asking for the possible uses of a particular indicator.

Class Materials:
Raw materials to prepare indicators
Water
200 mL beakers (or larger)
Funnel & filter paper
Large bottles to store final indicator
Heat source → hot plate or ring stand/ring/wire gauze with a Bunsen burner

Beaker tongs
Spot plates
Acidic solution (for example, vinegar)
Basic solution (for example, ammonia)

Materials for the teacher:
Larger funnel (if available)
Non-soluble markers (to label main storage bottles)

Preparation:
You may want to have stations where students can get the raw materials, and possibly large containers to collect the prepared indicator solutions.

During lab:
Circulate to observe students working and aid as necessary.

Pages to use for "Preparing pH Indicators":
Page 115 for a simple lab report.

Possible ChemMatters article:
Rohrig, Brian, "Paintball: Chemistry Hits Its Mark," ChemMatters, April, 2007, pp. 4-7, American Chemical Society.

This article describes the history of the sport of paintball and the requirements of producing the paintball itself.

This article is also a good supplement for the topics of **Hydrogen Bonding** and **Bond Polarity**.

Directions of how to get the article online are on Page 2.

Another option is a ChemMatters article on the CD ROM, but not online:
Ruth, Laura, "Aquarium Chemistry: Life in the Balance", ChemMatters, February, 2002, pp.6-7, American Chemical Society. This article describes the requirements and challenges of preparing an aquarium.

Sources:

http://www.woodrow.org/teachers/ci/1986/exp23.html

http://chemistry.about.com/cs/acidsandbases/a/aa060703a.htm

http://chemistry.about.com/od/acidsbase1/a/red-cabbage-ph-indicator.htm

http://www.chem.umn.edu/services/lecturedemo/info/Cabbage_Indicator.html

This article has directions for preparing red cabbage indicator.

http://antoine.frostburg.edu/chem/senese/101/acidbase/faq/natural-indicators.shtml

http://mypages.iit.edu/~smile/ch8622.html

D'Orso and Burnett, "Experimenter's Notebook: Mood Lipstick," ChemMatters December 1985, p.12, American Chemical Society.

Rohrig, Brian, "Paintball: Chemistry Hits Its Mark," ChemMatters, April, 2007, pp. 4-7, American Chemical Society.

Ruth, Laura, "Aquarium Chemistry: Life in the Balance", ChemMatters, February, 2002, pp.6-7, American Chemical Society.

Lab: Preparing pH Indicators

Name _____

Purpose:
To prepare and test acid-base indicators.

Materials:
Fruits and vegetables
Water
200 mL beakers (or larger)
Funnel & filter paper
Large bottles to store final indicator
Heat source → hot plate or ring stand/ring/wire gauze with a Bunsen burner

Beaker tongs
Spot plates
Acidic solution
Basic solution

Safety goggles are required.
Be cautious while heating the mixture and when pouring the heated solution.

Procedure:

Day 1:

1. Fill a 200 mL beaker approximately to the 50 mL mark with a chosen fruit or vegetable. Small pieces are best.
2. Fill the same beaker with water up to the 150 mL mark.
3. Set the beaker on the heat source. Once the mixture boils, boil for 10 minutes.
4. Turn off heat, and allow to cool for 10 minutes.
5. Set up another beaker with a funnel and folded filter paper.
6. Carefully, pour the solution through the filter paper.
7. Discard the filter paper and its contents.
8. Pour the filtered indicator solution in the class collection container.

For each indicator prepared, record the color of the raw material and the color of the solution.

If you've got more time, prepare a different indicator solution.

Day 2:
Using a spot plate, test all of the indicators prepared with an acid and a base.

Data

Indicator	Color of raw material	Color of solution	Color in acid	Color in base
1.				
2.				
3.				

Lab: Coinium

Summary
Student simulates radioactive decay of a radioisotope by flipping pennies in a covered box. The resulting data is analyzed. Students can work alone or in pairs.

Student Skills:
Graphing data that simulates nuclear half-life

Lab: Coinium — Teacher Information Page

Background:

This lab simulates nuclear half-life and produces data for analysis. For a class of 24 students, you'll need 1200 pennies ($12.00). Fortunately, the pennies can be obtained at a local bank and can be reused year after year. You may already have a penny collection at home or you can ask students and teachers to donate them.

This lab does call for a box with a lid per pair of students. A shoebox is very useful for this purpose and students can donate them to the class. I once performed this lab with cafeteria trays that were available, we just made sure to shake the trays up and down to prevent the pennies flying out the sides.

Class Materials:
1,200 pennies (100 for 2 students, this is enough for 12 pairs of students)
12 Boxes with lids

Materials for the teacher:
Nothing past the class materials.

Preparation:
Collect the boxes and pennies. You may wish to put groups of 100 pennies into plastic bags before the lab. This will save lab time and provide for easier storage for the next year. Students should count the pennies to make sure they have the correct number before they start.

During lab:
Monitor student progress and aid where appropriate.

Pages to use for "Coinium":
10 question report: pages 119-120.
Full write-up: pages 122-123.

Possible ChemMatters article:
McClure, Michael, "ChemHistory: The New Alchemy", ChemMatters, October, 2006, pp.15-17, American Chemical Society.

This article presents a history of formation of the elements, as well as the basics of **Radioactive Decay**, and it's an excellent overview of the basic concepts of **Nuclear Chemistry**.

This article is also a good supplement for the topic of the **History of Atomic Theory**. If I had to give it a grade, it's an A+ article!

Directions of how to get the article online are on Page 2.

Another excellent article:
Ruth, Carolyn, "Where Do Chemical Elements Come From?", ChemMatters, October, 2009, pp.6-8, American Chemical Society.
This article describes the formation of elements and compounds during a supernova explosion of a star.

Sources:

http://www.scienceteacherprogram.org/chemistry/stevens03.html

http://www.ncsu.edu/scivis/lessons/halflife/halflife2.html

http://mjksciteachingideas.com/pdf/HalfLifeLab.pdf

http://www.usoe.k12.ut.us/CURR/SCIENCE/sciber00/8th/earth/sciber/radioact.htm

http://www.freemathhelp.com/asymptotes.html

Pelletier, Ceanne et al., "Experiment 9-1: Understanding Half-life," Chemistry: Laboratory Experiments, D.C. Heath and Company, 1993.

McClure, Michael, "ChemHistory: The New Alchemy", ChemMatters, October, 2006, pp.15-17, American Chemical Society.

Ruth, Carolyn, "Where Do Chemical Elements Come From?", ChemMatters, October, 2009, pp.6-8, American Chemical Society.

Lab: Coinium   Name _____

Purpose:
To simulate radioactive decay, collect the data and analyze it.

Materials:
100 pennies   Box with cover

Procedure:
1. Place 100 pennies all heads up in the box.
2. Put on the cover and shake the box three times. Remove the cover.
3. Remove the atoms that have decayed (the pennies that have flipped to tails). Record the number of atoms that decayed and the number of atoms that remain.
4. Repeat steps 2 & 3. Continue trials until only 1 atom remains undecayed.

Data:

#1. Half-Life Number	#2. Number of atoms decayed in this half-life	#3. Number of Atoms remaining undecayed	#4. Total number of Atoms Decayed
0	0	100	0
1			
2			
3			
4			
5			
6			
7			
8			
9			
10			

Graphs -- Draw a smooth curve for each graph (Y-axis vs. X-axis).

1. Number of Atoms Decayed vs. Half-life (#2 vs. #1)

2. Total Number of Atoms Decayed vs. Half-life (#4 vs. #1)

Questions

Answer these questions on your own paper using full sentences -- rewrite the question or incorporate it into your answer.

1. Attach a copy of the first graph, Number of Atoms Decayed vs. Half-life, and describe its shape at the bottom of the page.

2. Scientists describe the stability of an isotope by reporting its half-life. Half-life is the amount of time required for one-half of a radioactive sample to decay. What is the "half-life" of your pennies?

3. How many pennies would you expect to remain undecayed after 4 Half-lives? Explain your answer.

4. Attach a copy of the second graph, Total number atoms decayed vs. Half-life, and describe its shape at the bottom of the page.

5. How many half-lives would it take for approximately 75 pennies to decay? Explain your answer.

6. How many half-lives would it take to have 1/8th as many pennies as you started? Explain your answer.

7. Is the quantity of a radioactive isotope ever exactly zero? Explain your answer.

8. Suppose you have a radioactive isotope with a half-life of two years and you start with 800 grams of this substance.
   a. How much of the original isotope will you have in two years?
   b. How much of the original isotope will you have in eight years?

9. The half-life of iodine-125 is 60 days. The half-life of iodine-131 is 8.05 days. Radioactive iodine is used as a tracer to help identify diseases of the thyroid gland. Which of these two isotopes would you choose to use on a patient? Explain your answer.

10. Evaluate the quality of your results and describe how you would improve this lab using the same or similar materials.

Answer Key for "Coinium":

1. A graph of Number of Atoms Decayed vs. Half-life is a decreasing parabola that is a horizontal asymptote.

2. The answer will depend on sample data, but can be verified with either graph. Ideally, 1 flip would equal 1 half-life, but it doesn't always correspond perfectly.

3. After 4 Half-lives, approximately 6 pennies would remain (rounding down).

    Fraction remaining = $\frac{1}{2}$ (total time elapsed/half-life) = $\frac{1}{2}$ (number of half-lives)

    Fraction remaining = $\frac{1}{2}^4 = \frac{1}{2} \times \frac{1}{2} \times \frac{1}{2} \times \frac{1}{2} = 1/16$

    100 x 1/16 = 6.25

4. A graph of the Total Number Atoms Decayed vs. Half-life is an increasing parabola that is a vertical asymptote.

5. The answer will depend on sample data, but can be verified with either graph. Ideally, 2 half-lives.

6. $\frac{1}{2} \times \frac{1}{2} \times \frac{1}{2} = 1/8$ → After 3 half-lives, 1/8 of the pennies would remain undecayed.

7. The total atoms remaining approaches, but never reaches, zero. The asymptote shown on the graph of Number of Atoms Decayed vs. Half-life demonstrates this.

8. a. 1 half-life, $\frac{1}{2}$ x 800 g = 400 grams
    b. 8 yrs x 1 half-life/2 years = 4 half-lives
    $\frac{1}{2} \times \frac{1}{2} \times \frac{1}{2} \times \frac{1}{2} = 1/16$
    1/16 x 800g = 50 grams

9. Iodine-131 would be the best to use because it has the shorter half-life of 8.05 days, and would undecayed in the body for a shorter time.

10. Answers will vary, but many students will cite the limitation of pennies compared to a true radioactive substance.

Lab: Coinium   Name _____

Purpose:
To simulate radioactive decay, collect the data and analyze it.

Materials:
100 pennies   Box with cover

Procedure:
1. Place 100 pennies all heads up in the box.
2. Put on the cover and shake the box three times. Remove the cover.
3. Remove the atoms that have decayed (the pennies that have flipped to tails). Record the number of atoms that decayed and the number of atoms that remain.
4. Repeat steps 2 & 3. Continue trials until only 1 atom remains undecayed.

Data:

#1. Half-Life Number	#2. Number of atoms decayed in this half-life	#3. Number of Atoms remaining undecayed	#4. Total number of Atoms Decayed
0	0	100	0
1			
2			
3			
4			
5			
6			
7			
8			
9			
10			

Graphs -- Draw a smooth curve for each graph (Y-axis vs X-axis).

1. Number of Atoms Decayed vs. Half-life (#2 vs. #1)

2. Total Number of Atoms Decayed vs. Half-life (#4 vs. #1)

Laboratory Report Requirements

Label and skip a line between each section. Data tables and charts attached on separate pages are to be labeled (ex. Data Table – see attached).

Title
Purpose
Materials
Procedure

Data -- Chart attached.

Graphs

Conclusion
In paragraph form, discuss the following ideas:

- Describe the shapes of the first graph, Number of Atoms Decayed vs. Half-Life. Describe the shape the second graph, Total Number Atoms Decayed vs. Half-life.

- Scientists describe the stability of an isotope by reporting its half-life. Half-life is the amount of time required for one-half of a radioactive sample to decay. What is the "half-life" of your pennies based on these two graphs? Explain your answer.

- Evaluate the quality of your results. Describe how you would improve this lab using the same or similar materials.

- The half-life of iodine-125 is 60 days. The half-life of iodine-131 is 8.05 days. Radioactive iodine is used as a tracer to help identify diseases of the thyroid gland. Which of these two isotopes would you choose to use on a patient? Explain your answer.

Lab: Preparing a Cross-Linked Polymer

Summary
Student prepares two different cross-linked polymer samples with glue, water and sodium borate solution by changing the glue/water ratio. The two samples are tested for ability to stretch, bounce and puddle.

Student Skills:
Preparation of two cross-linked polymers and observation of their properties

Lab: Preparing a Cross-Linked Polymer — Teacher Information Page

Background:
White glue contains polyvinyl acetate which is a liquid polymer. The borax links the polyvinyl acetate molecules to each other creating one large, flexible polymer. Students may have already experienced making this polymer (calling it "slime"). This experiment tests two samples prepared with different ratios of glue and water.

You can purchase sodium tetraborate ($Na_2B_4O_7$), or borax, in the laundry section of your local grocery store.

The saturated borax solution does not need to be added to the glue in a precise amount. If Beral pipets or eyedroppers are not available, pouring small portions of the borax solution can be accomplished with a small 50ml beaker, a graduated cylinder, or even a paper cup that has been folded to make a spout.

White glue can be purchased in a large container as well as 6-8 smaller containers. The small can be used and refilled as necessary. The cups and stirring rods end up as garbage so I recommend 150 – 300 mL plastic cups and solid, wooden stirring rods such as those used for coffee.

If time is an issue, one lab partner or lab group could prepare the slime with 10 mL of water and another partner/group make the slime with 20 mL of water.

Class Materials:
White glue
Small plastic cups (150 - 300 mL)
Beral pipets (if available)
Food coloring (if desired)
Ziploc bags

Sodium tetraborate solution ($Na_2B_4O_7$)
Wooden stirrers
Graduated cylinders
Non water soluble markers

Materials for the teacher:
Storage bottle for the sodium tetraborate solution.

Preparation:
To mix saturated sodium tetraborate solution, add enough solid sodium tetraborate to water until it no longer dissolves. Have some of the solid remaining at the bottom of the container because it shows that it is a saturated solution.

During lab:
Observe students and aid with supplies as necessary.

Pages to use for "Preparing a Cross-Linked Polymer":
10 question report: pages 127-128.
Full write-up: pages 130-131.

Possible ChemMatters article:
Washam, Cynthia, "Plastics Go Green", ChemMatters, April, 2010, pp.10-12, American Chemical Society.

This article describes the pros and cons of plant-based plastics (or bioplastics) and the future of research on bioplastics.

Directions of how to get the article online are on Page 2.

Another possible article:
Sitzman, Barbara and Goode, Regis, "Open for Discussion: Hand Sanitizers, Soaps, and Antibacterial Agents -- the Dirt on Getting Clean", ChemMatters, December, 2011, p. 5, American Chemical Society.
This article provides an overview of hand cleaning products used during the cold/flu season. Some structural **Organic Formulas** are used.

Sources:
http://portal.acs.org/portal/PublicWebSite/education/resources/highschool/chemmatters/CTP_005402

http://www.pkwy.k12.mo.us/west/teachers/anderson/pack10/labslime.pdf

http://www.r-scc.com/PDF/Tech-electronics.pdf

http://www.stevespanglerscience.com/experiment/00000039

http://www.madsci.org/experiments/archive/878680114.Ch.html

http://www.hometrainingtools.com/slime-recipes-project/a/1660/

http://scifun.chem.wisc.edu/chemweek/polymers/polymers.html

Washam, Cynthia, "Plastics Go Green", ChemMatters, April, 2010, pp.10-11, American Chemical Society.

Sitzman, Barbara and Goode, Regis, "Hand Sanitizers, Soaps, and Antibacterial Agents: the Dirt on Getting Clean", ChemMatters, December, 2011, p. 5, American Chemical Society.

Lab: Preparing a Cross-Linked Polymer

Name _____

Purpose:
To prepare a cross-linked polymer and observe its properties.

Materials:
White glue
Small plastic cups (150 - 300 mL)
Beral pipets
Food coloring (if desired)
Ziploc bags

Sodium tetraborate solution ($Na_2B_4O_7$)
Wooden stirrers
Graduated cylinder
Non water soluble marker

Procedure:

1. Fill a paper cup with 20 mL of water. Draw a line on the cup to mark the water's volume and pour it out. Fill the cup to the line with white glue.
2. Add 10 mL of water to the cup and stir the mixture for 30 seconds.
3. Add 1-2 drops of food coloring and stir.
4. While stirring, add drops of saturated sodium tetraborate solution until the mixture forms a solid mass.
5. Remove solid from cup. Rinse under water, lightly blot dry, and test for the ability to (a) stretch, (b) bounce and (c) puddle.

To make the 2nd polymer sample, use a new cup and prepare the polymer as in Steps #1-5 but using 10 mL of glue and 20 mL of water.

Qualitative Observations:

Slime made with 10mL of water: _____
_____
_____

Slime made with 20mL of water: _____
_____
_____

Rate your "Slime"
E = Excellent, G = Good, F = Fair, P = Poor

Volume of water (ml)	Ability to Stretch	Ability to Bounce	Ability to Puddle
10			
20			

Questions

Answer these questions on your own paper using full sentences -- either rewrite the question or incorporate it into your answer.

1. Describe the physical properties of the white glue used.

2. Describe the physical properties of the cross-linked polymer formed.

3. Explain if adding more sodium tetraborate to the slime changes the polymer produced

4. Based on the results for ability to stretch, bounce and puddle, describe the cross-linked polymer made with 10mL of water.

5. Based on the results for ability to stretch, bounce and puddle, describe the cross-linked polymer made with 20 mL of water.

6. State one possible reason that the two polymers prepared have different properties.

7. Evaluate the quality of your two cross-linked polymer samples.

8. Describe how you would improve this lab using the same or similar materials.

9. Using the same lab materials, describe how to make a polymer that stretches further without breaking.

10. List three examples of cross-linked polymers.

Answer Key for "Preparing a Cross-Linked Polymer":

1. The glue is a white, viscous liquid.

2. The cross-linked polymer is a solid that stretches but will break apart into pieces. The pieces of cross-linked polymer will rejoin to form a single mass, similar to a liquid.

3. Yes, adding more sodium tetraborate cross-links more of the glue to form a cross-linked polymer (slime). After all of the glue has reacted, there is excess sodium tetraborate that is later rinsed away.

4. The cross-linked polymer made with 10 mL of water bounces better than that made with 20 mL of water, but does not stretch or puddle as well.

5. The cross-linked polymer made with 20 mL of water stretches and puddles better than that made with 10 mL of water, but it does not bounce as well.

6. The two polymers have different properties because they were prepared with glue/ water mixtures of different ratios.

7. Answers will vary, but there were limits in the accuracy of measuring the glue volume because it was not measured in a graduated cylinder. Also, only one sample of slime made with each glue/water ratio was tested.

8. Answers will vary, but using a different measurement system for the volume of glue is one improvement.

9. Using more water (for example, 25 mL) in the glue makes the polymer stretch further before breaking.

10. Answers will vary, but possibilities include rubber, spandex and DNA.

Lab: Preparing a Cross-Linked Polymer   Name _____

Purpose:
To prepare a cross-linked polymer and observe its properties.

Materials:
White glue
Small plastic cups (150 - 300 mL)
Beral pipets
Food coloring (if desired)
Ziploc bags

Sodium tetraborate solution ($Na_2B_4O_7$)
Wooden stirrers
Graduated cylinder
Non water soluble marker

Procedure:

1. Fill a paper cup with 20 mL of water. Draw a line on the cup to mark the water's volume and pour it out. Fill the cup to the line with white glue.
2. Add 10 mL of water to the cup and stir the mixture for 30 seconds.
3. Add 1-2 drops of food coloring and stir.
4. While stirring, add drops of saturated sodium tetraborate solution until the mixture forms a solid mass.
5. Remove solid from cup. Rinse under water, lightly blot dry, and test for the ability to (a) stretch, (b) bounce and (c) puddle.

To make the 2nd polymer sample, use a new cup and prepare the polymer as in Steps #1-5 but using 10 mL of glue and 20 mL of water.

Qualitative Observations:

Slime made with 10mL of water: _____

_____

_____

Slime made with 20mL of water: _____

_____

_____

Rate your "Slime"
E = Excellent, G = Good, F = Fair, P = Poor

Volume of water (ml)	Ability to Stretch	Ability to Bounce	Ability to Puddle
10			
20			

Laboratory Report Requirements

Label and skip a line between each section. Data tables and charts attached on separate pages are to be labeled (ex. Data Table – see attached)

Title

Purpose

Materials

Procedure

Data

Conclusion

In paragraph form, discuss the following ideas:

- Which of the two cross-linked polymers prepared a) stretched better? b) bounced better? c) puddled better?

- Explain why the two cross-linked polymers prepared have different properties.

- Evaluate the quality of your results.

- Describe how you would improve this lab using the same or similar materials.

Lab: Salt and Ice Cream?

Summary
Students use ice and salt to freeze a mixture of cream, sugar and vanilla to prepare ice cream.

Student Skills:
Observing the freezing point depression of water (the solvent) by using salt (the solute)

Lab: Salt and Ice Cream? — Teacher Information Page

Background:
This is a good activity during the later days of the year as summer approaches.

I've performed a lab based on the principle of freezing point depression which prepared ice cream using Ziploc bags to hold the ice and salt. The ice cream didn't form in the lab period and we had to throw it out.

I did not try to make ice cream with salt and ice again until I encountered the **Play and Freeze Ice Cream Maker**.

The Play and Freeze Ice Cream Maker has a larger plastic ball that can be filled with ice and salt and an internal container to hold the cream, sugar and vanilla. The ball is passed and rolled (a good activity for students) and after 20-30 minutes, ice cream is the result. When I was introduced to this I observed that it was much neater than the Ziploc bag version of the lab.

There is a one-time cost for purchasing the Play and Freeze Ice Cream Maker but it is a good investment for your classroom or science department.

As of this writing, the pint size Play & Freeze Ice Cream Maker is $25.00 and the quart size is $33.00 at amazon.com (plus tax and shipping).

I recommend 3 pint size Play & Freeze Ice Cream Makers for a group of 24 students (3 x $25 = $75 plus tax) or 2 quart size Play & Freeze Ice Cream Makers for a group of 24 students (2 x $33 = $66 plus tax).

The science department or the class can contribute to the consumable materials (cream, sugar, vanilla, paper cups, plastic spoons, ice and rock salt).

A major laboratory safety rule is not to eat or drink in the chemistry laboratory, so the experiment must be performed outside of the lab. Alternate locations include a lecture room, a classroom kitchen (such as in the consumer science area), or outside (especially during the last days of school).

Class Materials:
Play and Freeze Ice Cream Maker(s)
Half & Half, Sugar, Vanilla → amounts listed below
Rock salt
2 Large wooden spoons
Two large plastic measuring cups
25 Paper cups
Ice cream toppings
Ice
Cooler (for ice)
25 Plastic spoons
Paper towels
Bowl

For one pint-sized Play & Freeze:
1 ½ cups half & half
1 tsp. vanilla
1/4 cup sugar

For one quart sized Play & Freeze:
3 cups half & half
1 ½ tsp. vanilla
2/3 cup sugar

These amounts have been reduced from the given recipe to allow for the expansion of the water in the mixture as it freezes.

For each Play and Freeze Ice Cream Maker (P&F Maker), the following four jobs are to be assigned:
- "Chefs" measure and put ice cream ingredients into the P&F Maker.
- "Chillers" measure and insert the ice and salt into the P&F Maker.
- "Shakers" get the class to move the P&F Maker for 10-15 minutes.
- "Stirrers" open the P&F Maker and stir the ice cream after 10-15 minutes and 20-30 minutes. After the 2nd "shaking", they stir the ice cream and serve it to the students.

Each job should be completed by two or more students. The teacher will have to determine how many students for each job depending on the class materials and class time. The Chefs and Chillers can work simultaneously (another time saver).

It is left to the teacher's discretion how to assign these jobs. Possible approaches include (a) the teacher chooses the job for each student, (b) the students volunteer for the various jobs, or (c) the student names are picked randomly.

To save time, especially if your class moves to an alternate location and/or meets for only 40 to 45 minutes, assign the jobs during the previous class session.

Preparation:
Make arrangements for the alternate location for the class. Ideally, your class would have access to a sink for the water and salt disposal and for cleaning of the materials later.

Ask the head of your science department, or contact the school's main office, regarding procedures for taking the class to another location. If possible, store the ice cream materials in that location. If you have to meet in your regular classroom and then move to that alternate location, you may want to measure the cream, vanilla and sugar ahead to save time.

If a refrigerator is not available, use a camping cooler. Bowls, spoons and measuring cups can be obtained at the local dollar store, or they might be borrowed from the Consumer Science Department. Also, decide if you are going to wash the materials on site or bring them to the consumer/food science area to wash.

During Lab:
Supervise the progress of each group and aid where appropriate. The P&F Maker will not bounce but will simply crack. Warn students not to bounce the P&F Maker like a basketball.

Watch the clock to make sure the class finishes with enough time to eat!

Pages to use for "Salt in Ice Cream?":
10 question report: pages 136-137.
Full write-up: pages 139-140.

Possible ChemMatters article:
Kimbrough, Doris R., "Salting Roads: The Solution for Winter Driving", ChemMatters February, 2006, pp.14-16, American Chemical Society.

This article describes how salt, which causes **Freezing Point Depression** in water, is used to control ice on winter roads.

Directions of how to get the article online are on Page 2.

Sources:

http://www.icecreamrevolution.com/

http://www.squidoo.com/ice-cream-ball-maker-information
This has a video to show how the ice cream ball can be used.

http://chemistry.about.com/cs/howtos/a/aa020404a.htm

http://faculty.chemeketa.edu/jcammack/CH105/CH105%20Labs/11%20CH105%20Colligative%20Properties.pdf

http://www.cpet.ufl.edu/BestPractices/PDF/Physical%20Science/Energy%20Transfer%20and%20Transformations/Thermodynamics%20of%20Making%20Ice%20Cream-%20Exploring%20Heat%20and%20Colligative%20Properties%20of%20matter.pdf

http://www.waycross.edu/faculty/bmajdi/coligative%20properties%20of%20ice%20cream.htm

http://www.foodsci.uoguelph.ca/dairyedu/findsci.html

https://www.msu.edu/~weissmi1/icecream.htm

http://chemed.chem.purdue.edu/genchem/topicreview/bp/ch15/colligative.php

Wilbraham, Antony et al., Chemistry, Fifth Edition, Prentice Hall, 2000, Menlo Park, CA.

Field, Simon Quellan, Why There's Antifreeze in Your Toothpaste: The Chemistry of Household Ingredients, Chicago Review Press, 2008.

Kimbrough, Doris R., "Salting Roads: The Solution for Winter Driving", ChemMatters February, 2006, pp.14-16, American Chemical Society.

Lab: Salt and Ice Cream?

Name _____

Job: _____

Purpose:
To prepare ice cream using the freezing point depression of water (the solvent) and rock salt (the solute).

Materials:
Play and Freeze Ice Cream Maker(s) w/ plastic wrench
Cream   Sugar
Vanilla   Ice
Rock salt   Spoons
Bowl   Cups
Measuring cups and spoon

Procedure:
1. See your teacher about getting your job for this lab.
2. The "Chillers" fill the ice end of the Play and Freeze Ice Cream Maker with as much ice as possible and put in about ¾ cup of rock salt, and hand tighten the lid.
3. The "Chefs" combine the cream, sugar and vanilla in a large measuring cup. See your teacher for the amounts to use. The "Chefs" pour the mixture into the end of the ice cream maker with the metal cylinder. There should be about an inch of space above the mixture to allow for its expansion. Hand tighten the lid.
4. The "Shakers" are in charge of getting the group of students to pass the ball around to mix the ingredients.
5. After the ball is moved for about 10-15 minutes, the "Stirrers" open the ice cream end of the ball using the plastic wrench. Scrape the sides of the cylinder to mix up the ice cream using a plastic or wooden spoon. Replace the lid and tighten it by hand.
6. The "Chillers" check the ice end. Pour out the excess water into a sink and add more ice and up to 1/3 cup more rock salt to continue freezing the ice cream. Close the lid securely.
7. The "Shakers" make sure the ball is passed around to mix the ingredients for another 10-15 minutes.
8. The "Stirrers" open the ice cream end, stir and spoon the ice cream into a large bowl. The class can eat and enjoy what they made!

Qualitative Observations:
1. Ingredients before being placed in the ice cream maker:

_____
_____
_____

2. Ingredients after 20 to 30 minutes in the ice cream maker:

_____
_____

Questions
Answer these questions on your own paper using full sentences -- either rewrite the question or incorporate it into your answer.

1. State the definition of **colligative property** and state two examples.

2. State the definition of **vapor pressure.**

3. Explain how a dissolved solute affects vapor pressure.

4. What will happen to the freezing point of water (ice) after you put salt in it?

5. What will happen to the boiling point of water after you put salt in it?

6. The salt and ice mixture you used to cool your ice cream felt cold. Is melting of ice an endothermic or exothermic process? Explain your answer.

7. Which of the following 1 molal solutions would have the lowest freezing point, NaCl, $BaCl_2$, $AlCl_3$, $KClO_2$? Explain your answer and write the dissolution equation for your answer including phases.

8. Explain why a 1 molar solution of the molecular solid sucrose would not make an ice water mixture as cold as a 1 molar solution containing the ionic NaCl.

9. What is the freezing point constant of water? What is the boiling point constant of water? (Include units in both answers.)

10. Show the calculation and answer for the freezing point of a solution that contains 1.25 moles of a nonvolatile, nonelectrolyte solute in 0.750 kg water.

Answer Key for "Salt and Ice Cream?":

1. A **colligative property** is a property of a solution that depends on the concentration of the solute particles. Two examples of colligative properties are boiling point elevation and freezing point depression.

2. **Vapor Pressure** is the pressure produced when vaporized particles above the liquid in a sealed container collide with the container walls.

3. A dissolved solute lowers the surface area occupied by pure solvent, causing fewer particles of the solvent to evaporate and lowering the vapor pressure.

4. The freezing point temperature of water (ice) will be lowered after combination with salt.

5. The boiling point temperature of water will be higher after combination with salt.

6. The melting of ice is an endothermic process as energy is absorbed by the ice/salt mixture to melt it.

7. Aluminum chloride ($AlCl_3$) would have the lowest freezing point because it would produce 4 ions per particle dissolved, while NaCl would produced 2 ions per particle dissolved, $BaCl_2$ would produce 3 ions per particle, and $KClO_2$ would produce 3 ions per particle as well.

$$AlCl_3 (s) \leftrightarrow Al^{3+} (aq) + 3\, Cl^{1-} (aq)$$

8. An equal concentration of molecular solid sucrose would not make an ice water mixture as cold as one with sodium chloride because the sucrose does not break apart into more particles, or ionize, when it dissolves.

9. The freezing point constant of water is -1.86 °C for every 1 mole of particles in 1000 grams of water (°C / molal). The boiling point constant of water is 0.512 °C for every 1 mole of particles in 1000 grams of water (°C / molal).

10. Molality = moles solute / kg solvent

    Molality = 1.25 moles solute / 0.750 kg water

    Molality = 1.67 moles/kg = 1.67 molal

    $\Delta T_f = K_f \times$ molal

    Change in freezing point = freezing point constant x molality

    ΔT_f = (1.86 °C/molal) x 1.67 molal = 3.11 °C

    0 °C (freezing point of water) – 3.11 °C = -3.11 °C

Lab: Salt and Ice Cream?　　　　　Name _____

　　　　　　　　　　　　　　　　　　　Job: _____

Purpose:
To prepare ice cream using the freezing point depression of water (the solvent) and rock salt (the solute).

Materials:
Play and Freeze Ice Cream Maker(s) w/ plastic wrench
Cream　　　　　　　　　　　　　Sugar
Vanilla　　　　　　　　　　　　　Ice
Rock salt　　　　　　　　　　　　Spoons
Bowl　　　　　　　　　　　　　　Cups
Measuring cups and spoon

Procedure:
1. See your teacher about getting your job for this lab.
2. The "Chillers" fill the ice end of the Play and Freeze Ice Cream Maker with as much ice as possible and put in about ¾ cup of rock salt, and hand tighten the lid.
3. The "Chefs" combine the cream, sugar and vanilla in a large measuring cup. See your teacher for the amounts to use. The "Chefs" pour the mixture into the end of the ice cream maker with the metal cylinder. There should be about an inch of space above the mixture to allow for its expansion. Hand tighten the lid.
4. The "Shakers" are in charge of getting the group of students to pass the ball around to mix the ingredients.
5. After the ball is moved for about 10-15 minutes, the "Stirrers" open the ice cream end of the ball using the plastic wrench. Scrape the sides of the cylinder to mix up the ice cream using a plastic or wooden spoon. Replace the lid and tighten it by hand.
6. The "Chillers" check the ice end. Pour out the excess water into a sink and add more ice and up to 1/3 cup more rock salt to continue freezing the ice cream. Close the lid securely.
7. The "Shakers" make sure the ball is passed around to mix the ingredients for another 10-15 minutes.
8. The "Stirrers" open the Ice cream end, stir and spoon the ice cream into a large bowl. The class can eat and enjoy what they made!

Qualitative Observations:
1. Ingredients before being placed in the ice cream maker:

_____
_____
_____

2. Ingredients after 20 to 30 minutes in the ice cream maker:

_____
_____
_____

Laboratory Report Requirements

Label and skip a line between each section. Data tables and charts attached on separate pages are to be labeled (ex. Data Table – see attached)

Title

Purpose

Materials

Procedure

Data   Write "See Attached" and attach the completed lab handout.

Conclusion

In paragraph form, discuss the following ideas:

- State the definition of colligative property and state two examples of colligative properties.

- The salt and ice mixture you used to cool your ice cream felt cold. Is melting of ice an endothermic or exothermic process? Explain your answer.

- Which of the following 1 molal solutions would have the lowest freezing point, NaCl, $BaCl_2$, $AlCl_3$, $KClO_2$? Explain your answer and write the dissolution equation including phases.

- Show the calculation and answer for the freezing point of a solution that contains 1.25 moles of nonvolatile, nonelectrolyte solute in 0.750 kg water.

Postlogue

I hope this book is a practical addition to your repertoire as a Chemistry teacher. Consult the teachers in your science department for other laboratory activities that have traditionally been performed such as the percent composition of water in a $CuSO_4$ hydrate sample or acid-base titration. The materials for these labs are either in the department or are easily obtained.

I welcome your feedback from using these labs.

Please send emails with the Re: Lab book feedback to: MarjHee13@yahoo.com

About the Author:

Marjorie R. Heesemann has a Bachelor of Arts in Chemistry from the University of Virginia, a Masters in Education from SUNY at Buffalo, and a 6th Year Certificate from the Institute of Science Instruction and Study (ISIS) program at Southern Connecticut State University.

After 15 years of teaching chemistry, she is now working to contribute her knowledge and experiences to developing resources for the Chemistry classroom. This text is her initial attempt at producing materials for the teacher. Marjorie R. Heesemann plans to produce videos/dvds for the chemistry classroom. Keep an eye out for a website in the future.

Index

Acid, 63-66, 68-72, 100-113, 115, 141

Aluminum foil, 6, 7, 9-12

Base, 100-112, 115

Best-fit line, 22, 25, 27, 28

Calorimetry, 82, 85, 88, 90-93, 96, 97

Candle, 90- 99

Chalkboard, 58, 60, 62

ChemMatters, 1, 2, 7, 15, 16, 24, 32, 41, 51, 58, 67, 75, 84, 92, 102, 113, 117, 118, 126, 135

Chromatography, 38-43, 45, 46

Colligative, 137, 138, 140

Density, 6, 9, 10, 12, 14-23, 25-29, 40, 83, 85-89, 94, 98

Filter paper, 31, 33-37, 39, 42, 45, 46, 113, 115

Freezing point, 132,133, 135-140

Half-life, 116, 117, 119-123

Heat of fusion, 82, 83, 85-89

Hydrochloric acid, 63, 65, 66, 68, 69, 71, 72

Indicator, 100 -113, 115

Lab assistant, 3, 4

Laboratory Safety Contract, 4

Law of Conservation of Energy, 82, 86, 87, 89

Molar volume, 3, 73-75, 77-81

Mole, 49, 50-52, 54, 55, 57, 58, 60-62, 66, 69, 70, 72, 73, 77-81, 137, 138, 140

Muriatic acid, 64-66

Percent error, 25, 30, 33, 34, 36, 37, 69, 70, 72, 73, 77-82, 86, 87, 89, 91, 94-96, 98, 99

Index (continued)

Polymer, 41, 124, 125, 127-131

Radioactive decay, 116, 117, 119, 122

Relative mass, 49, 50-56

Safety, 4, 15, 64-68, 71, 75, 77, 80, 93, 97, 103, 108, 115, 133

Significant figures, 6, 7, 9-12, 17, 20, 21

Specific heat, 85, 86, 88, 89, 91, 94, 96, 98

Thermometer, 1, 75, 77, 80, 83-85, 88, 91, 93, 97

Volume, 3, 6, 9-14, 17-22, 25-29, 40, 66, 73-75, 77-83, 85, 87, 88, 90, 127, 129, 130